1

Redemption

God's Eternal Purpose
through Jesus Christ

By David A. DePra

2

Table of Contents

Introduction

God has completely finished REDEMPION for the entire human race – in His Son. But the human race must repent and believe – the human race must enter into redemption by becoming those who are IN CHRIST. If we do, then we can discover Him. We can discover the fullness of God IN HIM, and experience the fullness of redemption IN HIM.

Redemption is not merely a matter of getting saved. Rather, it is the restoration of humanity back into relationship with God – and therefore the restoration of humanity back into the eternal plan and purpose of God through Jesus Christ. And it is also the gathering up of all things in Christ as Lord for His glory.

The intention of this book is to center ALL things in Christ – and show that He is not only the One who finished the redemption, but He is the One who IS our redemption.

Chapter 1
God's Living Word: Jesus Christ

God, who at sundry times and in divers manners spoke in time past unto the fathers by the prophets, Has in these last days spoken unto us by [his] Son. (Heb. 1:1-2)

The epistle to the Hebrews opens with such simplicity. Yet what is stated governs the entire epistle. Indeed, these words can be said to govern the entire purpose and plan of God for this age – as revealed elsewhere in scripture. Does that seem to be an exaggeration? It is not. If anything, it is an understatement.

Read the above words carefully – and in doing so, put aside all religious tradition. If possible, put aside natural understanding -- and HEAR those inspired Words.

Perhaps a closer look at the Greek will bring some clarity. The phrase, "by His Son," actually reads, "IN His Son." In other words, Jesus Christ did not merely convey to us the words of God. Rather, Jesus Christ IS the Word of God. And if we believe this opening statement of this epistle, despite all of the other words that God has spoken, God has spoken His FINAL Word – His COMPLETE Word – His LIVING Word – through the revelation of His Son, Jesus Christ.

This does NOT negate the Bible, or negate the ways and means by which God has otherwise spoken. Rather, in Christ all that God has spoken is gathered up into a Living Person – a Living Person that God desires to reveal IN believers.

Christianity is, "Christ in you, the hope of glory." (Col. 1:27) Christ IN believers is the source of ALL, and He is the end purpose of ALL – Jesus Christ is the LIFE of ALL. He is the Alpha and the Omega. This means that Christianity is an ongoing inward revelation and experience of the Person of Jesus Christ – through Whom we SEE and HEAR all the God will ever speak.

To put it another way, the Person of Jesus Christ IS the, "language," in which God is speaking today. An inward realization of Jesus Christ is WHO God is speaking -- and WHO we must hear.

This should not be surprising, for John wrote:

In the beginning was the Word, and the Word was with God, and the Word was God. The same was in the beginning with God. All things were made by him; and without him was not anything made that was made. In him was life; and the life was the light of men. (John 1:1-4)

Jesus Christ IS the Word of God – He is the LOGOS – He is the revelation that God has for humanity. Indeed, IN HIM is not only LIFE – but IN HIM is the LIGHT of men. All revelation that God has to give – indeed, ALL things that God has for humanity – are given IN, and given ONLY IN the Person of Jesus Christ.

In a very real sense, Jesus Christ IS the gospel — His Person, and all that He has done. Jesus Christ in believers — or if you prefer — believers in Jesus Christ — is the core of Christianity. Jesus Christ in believers is the church. Christ in His people is the New Covenant. And the inward revelation of Jesus Christ in His people is the ROCK upon which God builds ALL.

Jesus really is the Living Word of God. He is THE WORD that God is speaking. He is the ONLY WORD that God has ever spoken or ever will speak to humanity.

What we must grasp is that, yes, God is speaking doctrines and teachings ABOUT Christ. Those are always going to emerge, and rightly so. But those alone will not get us far. Rather than speak only facts, doctrines, and teachings ABOUT Christ, God is speaking — revealing — CHRIST HIMSELF. God is speaking the inward revelation of Jesus Christ within each believer. Therefore, we must hear. We must believe. We must ask God to do whatever it takes to open our ears and eyes to Christ.

Blindness and Unbelief

It is an unfortunate fact that despite the absolute Truth of Jesus Christ as THE WORD that God speaks — and despite the absolute fact that Christianity is CHRIST IN US — it is an unfortunate fact that this is a reality to which hundreds of millions of professing believers are blind. In fact, the suggestion itself is often met with resistance, if not antagonism. Is this not evidence that Satan has been at work?

One of the most common objections to this great Truth is that it minimizes the written Word of God. That argument is utter nonsense – and it comes from ignorance to the Truth. The Bible is the written Truth of God. Jesus Christ is the Living Truth of God. The Bible is the written Word of God. Jesus Christ is the Living Word of God. But there is ONLY ONE TRUTH of God. There is ONLY ONE WORD of God. So obviously, the written and the Living MUST agree. Thus, all that God reveals in His Son – ALL that God speaks IN HIS SON – will agree completely with what is in the written Word. There are no exceptions. But what a shallow and dead Christianity emerges from living only in that which is written. Indeed, Paul wrote:

Who also hath made us able ministers of the new testament; not of the letter, but of the spirit: for the letter kills, but the spirit gives life. (II Cor. 3:6)

Note: The spirit gives LIFE. And Jesus Christ is THE LIFE – He is OUR life. (Col. 3:4) To reduce Christianity down to a creed – to a theological construct – will not get us far. It will result in dead religion.

The Jews were given the Word of God – the Old Testament. But the Old Testament was a type and a shadow of the Living Christ. If they had given themselves to God they would have seen this – they would have seen the One to Whom the OT pointed: Jesus Christ, the Messiah. But they would not abandon the religion THEY had created out of the Bible. In effect, they abandoned Christ Himself in favor of their religious tradition.

This people draws nigh unto me with their mouth, and honors me with [their] lips; but their heart is far from me. But in vain they do worship me, teaching [for] doctrines the commandments of men. (Matt. 15:8-9)

Ye have not his word abiding in you: for whom he hath sent, him ye believe not. Search the scriptures; for in them ye think ye have eternal life: and they are they which testify of me. And ye will not come to me, that ye might have life. (John 5:38-40)

Do we think that such a condition is impossible for professing believers in our modern churches? Do we think we are above all of that because we profess Christ, preach Christ, form churches, denominations, and ministries? The fact is, what was true for the Jews in the first century is true regarding the church – in an ever-growing way in our day. The reality of Jesus Christ within – the reality of Christ as our life – the plan and purpose of God that can only emerge from Him – hundreds of millions are blinded to Him. Hundreds of millions have never heard the ONE WORD God is today speaking: The Person of His Son. He has been replaced by religion ABOUT HIM. He has been replaced by intellectualism, emotionalism, or rank heresy.

Today God Speaks Christ

Read again those opening words of the epistle to the Hebrews. God, in times past, USED to speak through prophets – USED to speak through many different means. But IN THESE LAST DAYS....can we see that there is a contrast that is given? We are NOT told that God is today continuing to speak in the same ways in which He USED to speak. No. We are told that God used to speak through various means, BUT NOW -- "In these last days God is speaking to us IN HIS SON." He is speaking to us, "Son-wise." Jesus is Who God is speaking.

Hundreds of millions of sincere Christian people do not even know what that means. Many do not KNOW to care what it means. The church, by and large – has been blinded to Christ Himself. He is preached, yes, as the One who saved us, but when it comes to the means by which we are to live the Christian life He has been pushed aside in favor of other things. Such thinking is error. Jesus Christ is what God wants to do in our lives.

Paul travailed:

My little children, of whom I travail in birth again until Christ be formed in you. (Gal. 4:19)

Wherefore I also, after I heard of your faith in the Lord Jesus, and love unto all the saints, Cease not to give thanks for you, making mention of you in my prayers; That the God of our Lord Jesus Christ, the Father of glory, may give unto you the spirit of

wisdom and revelation in the knowledge of him: The eyes of your understanding being enlightened; that ye may know... (Eph. 1:15-18)

Here is see the heart cry of the apostle Paul – inspired by God – which means it is the heart cry of God Himself. God wants us to come into an inward realization of His Son – which is the meaning of, "Christ formed in believers." He wants us to KNOW HIM – which includes EXPERIENCING HIM. That is why God is speaking Jesus Christ. The question is whether we have ears to hear.

The issue here is not a theological one. Rather, the issue is one of spiritual life or death. Either we believe God is speaking Christ -- or we do not. Either we are opening our eyes and ears to the One Whom God is speaking -- or we are not. Either we are willing to abandon ourselves to God for whatever it takes -- or we or not. If we think we can sit on the fence, be lukewarm on this issue, or simply dismiss it as nonsense, we are deceived. Jesus Christ IS God's Word. There is NO other.

The Only Answer

There is only one solution to spiritual blindness, and it is never to see THINGS, Bible meanings, or religious interpretations. No. Those alone will not get us far. The only solution is to SEE JESUS. Once we see Jesus, we are no longer blind.

It is ironic that the greatest blindness is to be blind to the fact you are blind! The greatest blindness is to think that you see! Thus, the first step that God initiates is to make us aware that we are, in fact, blind. Isn't that, in a sense, SEEING? Sure. Then we have SEEN that we do not see – we have seen that we are blind. Then we can begin – we can begin to cry out, "Lord, that I may see! Lord, that I may hear."

Hearing and seeing are both pictures of spiritual realization. Our great need is to begin to come in to an inward seeing; into an inward realization of Jesus Christ. HE is the Light. HE is the Truth. He is the Living Word that God speaks.

Then, and only then, will the Bible come alive. We will see what the Bible MEANS when we see and hear the One about Whom the Bible speaks:

> *But their minds were blinded: for until this day remains the same veil untaken away in the reading of the old testament; which [veil] is done away in Christ. But even unto this day, when Moses is read, the veil is upon their heart. Nevertheless when it shall turn to the Lord, the veil shall be taken away. Now the Lord is that Spirit: and where the Spirit of the Lord [is], there [is] liberty. But we all, with open face beholding as in a glass the glory of the Lord, are changed into the same image from glory to glory, [even] as by the Spirit of the Lord.*
> *(II Cor. 3:14-18)*

The Word of God

God is today speaking IN HIS SON – through an ongoing inward realization of Jesus Christ. He is revealing Christ to individuals, in a personal, one-on-one, growing way. This is what God is doing in this age – unto His purposes, not only for this age -- but extending into the eternal ages to come.

We are not to, "hear," what God is speaking as a thing unto itself. "To hear," always means to be open to what is spoken – it means to give oneself over to what God is saying. Certainly, this means salvation. But that is only the beginning. God is speaking Christ for purpose salvation makes possible. He is speaking SONSHIP. He is speaking eternal INHERITANCE. He is speaking the full purpose that He intended for humanity before the foundation of the world. But ALL of this is found solely in the Person of Jesus Christ.

Christ is God's Word – the first, the last, and the ALL. If the church is going to experience Jesus Christ, and God's purpose through Him, the church needs to wake up and start to HEAR and embrace the ONE Whom God is speaking.

God's revelation of the Living Jesus Christ will ALWAYS completely agree with scripture – in fact, scripture itself says that God is speaking Christ and revealing Christ to individuals. Yet it does not matter how loudly we shout that the Bible is the written Truth of God and will ALWAYS agree with God revelation of the Living Truth – there will be those who say this is a denial of God's inspired written Word. This betrays a blindness to the Living Word. Therein is the problem in much of the church today.

13

Chapter 2
God's Purpose for Humanity

When we think of the Redemption of Jesus Christ, we tend to limit it to what Jesus did to save the human race. And without a doubt, that is central. But the Redemption goes far beyond that. The Redemption of Jesus Christ was the means by which God restored, and is restoring, the entire creation back under Himself through His Son as Lord of all.

At the center of God's redemptive plan was the human race. The salvation of those who turn to Christ is central to God's plan because it is through THE SON -- and then through sons and daughters IN THE SON -- that God intends to work out His full purpose.

And if children, then heirs; heirs of God, and joint-heirs with Christ; if so be that we suffer with [him], that we may be also glorified together. For I reckon that the sufferings of this present time [are] not worthy [to be compared] with the glory which shall be revealed in us. For the earnest expectation of the creature waits for the manifestation of the sons of God. (Rom. 8:17-19)

For it became him, for whom [are] all things, and by whom [are] all things, in bringing many sons unto glory, to make the captain of their salvation perfect through sufferings. For both he that sanctifies and they who are sanctified [are] all of one: for which cause

he is not ashamed to call them brethren,
Saying, I will declare thy name unto my
brethren, in the midst of the church will I
sing praise unto thee. And again, I will put
my trust in him. And again, Behold I and the
children which God hath given me. (Heb.
2:10-13)

Jesus Christ is to be Lord over all creation, and those who are IN CHRIST are intended by God to be living recipients of all that He is — resulting in them being living expressions and extensions of Him — throughout the eternal ages. This is the essential for inheritance and dominion.

Dominion

God originally gave the first man dominion over His creation. But once Adam sinned, God sent His Son to become THE MAN (the God-man) Who would receive that dominion and fulfill God's purpose. All who are IN CHRIST are destined to be coheirs in Him, under Him, and unto God's glory. We see this purpose upfront in the epistle to the Hebrews:

What is man, that thou art mindful of him?
or the son of man, that thou visit him? Thou
made him a little lower than the angels;
thou crowned him with glory and honor, and
didst set him over the works of thy hands:
Thou hast put all things in subjection under
his feet. For in that he put all in subjection
under him, he left nothing [that is] not put
under him. But now we see not yet all things
put under him. But we see Jesus, who was
made a little lower than the angels for the

15

suffering of death, crowned with glory and honor; that he by the grace of God should taste death for every man. (Heb. 2:6-9)

The key phrase in this passage is, "But we see Jesus." God created humanity for dominion under Himself. But we do not yet see this. Rather, WE SEE JESUS – Who is THE MAN (God become man) through Whom God's purpose for all of humanity will be fulfilled.

We must ALWAYS, "see Jesus." There is no plan or purpose of God except it be IN CHRIST – except it be in Christ NOW and FOREVER. All that God has done, or will ever do regarding His people, will result in all creation SEEING JESUS – Christ will be manifested; Christ will be all in all.

That in the dispensation of the fullness of times he might gather together in one all things in Christ, both which are in heaven, and which are on earth; [even] in him. (Eph. 1:10)

And hath put all [things] under his feet, and gave him [to be] the head over all [things] to the church, Which is his body, the fullness of him that fills all in all. (Eph. 1:22)

Now, with an understanding of God's original purpose for creating the human race, we can turn to that creation account in Genesis.

The Creation of Man

Let us make man in our image, after our likeness: and let them have dominion over

16

the fish of the sea, and over the fowl of the air, and over the cattle, and over all the earth, and over every creeping thing that creeps upon the earth. So God created man in his [own] image, in the image of God created he him; male and female created he them. And God blessed them, and God said unto them, Be fruitful, and multiply, and replenish the earth, and subdue it: and have dominion over the fish of the sea, and over the fowl of the air, and over every living thing that moves upon the earth. (Gen. 1:26-28)

And the LORD God formed man [of] the dust of the ground, and breathed into his nostrils the breath of life; and man became a living soul. (Gen. 2:7)

Note that the first man, although physically formed from the dust of the ground, was NOT alive until God Himself BREATHED into Him, "the breath of LIVES." The phrase, "breath of life," ought to be translated, "breath of LIVES." It is plural. Thus, both Adam's physical life and his spiritual life were directly breathed into him from God.

If you do some study on the words for breath, air, and spirit, you will find that in both the OT and NT the words are the same. The, "breath of God," is nothing more than the spirit of God. God "breathed," into Adam His spirit – and it was only at that point that Adam became a LIVING soul.

What is important to see about this is that the life of humanity – both the physical and spiritual life

17

– were originally out from the life of God Himself. God BREATHED these. Now, don't misunderstand. God did not breath into Adam DIVINITY. No. God breathed life that was of God – but was intended for human beings on the human level.

All that being said, can we see that when God breathed into Adam the breath of lives that this established an ONENESS OF LIFE between God and Adam? – a oneness that was intended to be maintained forever? We might say that God intended to be continually and forever breathing into Adam the breath of lives – Adam's life was to be continually derived from God as the source.

This is an important point. God did not give Adam life as a THING for Adam to possess within himself -- apart from God. Rather, God gave Adam HIMSELF – God intended Adam to forever be ONE with Himself. That communion was established when God breathed into Adam.

This becomes clear once Adam sinned. His oneness with God was severed – and death was the result. This would not have happened if Adam had possessed life within himself independent of God. No. Adam died because he severed the communion/breath of God. It was to be a continual relationship. Adam severed that through sin.

So right from the start we find that ALL life is from God. But also that ALL life is maintained from out of continual fellowship with God – life is continually given. God never intended for human beings to live independent of Himself. Human were to be alive because of a continual abiding in, and out from, God.

God's Normal

Most of us think that the human beings that we are, and that we see around us, are NORMAL. But the human race is NOT normal. Since the sin of Adam, the human race is ABNORMAL. It is abnormal because the oneness that God originally established at the creation was severed. In Jesus Christ, God has restored the NORMAL – and really much more. But the fullness of that will not be made manifest until the resurrection.

This means that we presently have little idea of the humanity that God originally created – we have little idea of God Himself. All we see is fallen humanity. And since we all look and act the same, we think that this ABNORMAL condition of humanity is NORMAL.

Now, in Jesus Christ, the Son of God become man, we do begin to see the NORMAL human being – according to God's mind. And we do have a revelation of God Himself. It is because Jesus became the NORMAL human being – sinless before God -- that IN CHRIST is redemption for the human race.

The Original Design of God

When God was finished with the original creation – when H finished creating the first human beings – the Bible gives this description:

***And they were both naked, the man and his
wife, and were not ashamed. (Gen. 2:25)***

This is a description of God's mind — of God's
original design for humanity. It is a description
of God's NORMAL. Human beings were created
and designed by God to BE NAKED, and yet not
ashamed. What does that mean?

To be, "naked," means to have nothing about
yourself — nothing in yourself — as a resource for
life. Left to yourself, you are utterly barren. You
are naked of ALL. But to be UNASHAMED of this
condition means that you are not aware of any
need. You are not aware of any need because
you are in fellowship with the One Who IS your
life; Who is the source of all that you need.

"Naked and unashamed," is God's will for all of
humanity. It is God's normal. And through Jesus
Christ it is God's intention to restore humanity
back to this original design and relationship. To
be, "naked and unashamed," is the outcome of
redemption in Jesus Christ.

God created Adam, and then Eve, from out of
Adam. And He saw that it was very good. God's
purpose was on course. But God also created
Adam and Eve with a free will. This would have
to be proven and built.

Chapter 3
The Sin of Adam

And the LORD God planted a garden eastward in Eden; and there he put the man whom he had formed. And out of the ground made the LORD God to grow every tree that is pleasant to the sight, and good for food; the tree of life also in the midst of the garden, and the tree of knowledge of good and evil. (Gen. 2:8-9)

And the LORD God commanded the man, saying, Of every tree of the garden thou may freely eat: But of the tree of the knowledge of good and evil, thou shall not eat of it: for in the day that thou eat thereof thou shall surely die. (Gen. 2:16)

God is the source of all life. He was the continual source of life for Adam. This fact is represented by the TREE OF LIFE. Eating of the TREE OF LIFE is symbolic of Adam living in fellowship with God — it is symbolic of Adam of Adam continually deriving his breath of life from God Himself. As long as Adam lived in and out from God has his life he was, "naked and unashamed." He was NORMAL. He was walking in the purpose of God.

But not only is God the source of all LIFE, but He is likewise the source of all LIGHT. God is LIGHT. God is TRUTH. Thus, God intended Adam to know good from evil -- by knowing God Himself.

21

Here we see WHY eating of the, "tree of the knowledge of good and evil," was forbidden. It was certainly not because God forbade Adam to discern good from evil. Hardly, for God was revealing to Adam good from evil in the commands He was giving to Adam. And to know God and be in fellowship with God is going to automatically give a person a discernment of good and evil. In other words, if you know God you will know what is OF Him, and what is NOT of Him. But notice: To eat of this forbidden tree constituted a choice to decide for ONESELF what was good and what was evil. It was, in effect, a choice to possess life for oneself – rather than from out of fellowship with God. It was a choice to decide for oneself good and evil – rather than from out of knowing God. It was, in effect, a declaration of independence from God. It was a violation of fellowship with God, and a severing from the very purpose for which Adam was created.

We read the commands of God. He told Adam that if he ate of the forbidden tree that, "in the day that you eat thereof, you shall surely die." Can we see why? God is LIFE. Thus, to eat of the forbidden tree constituted a severing of Adam from God as his LIFE. The result was death.

Satan knew this would be the result. So, he approached Eve. And therein we find the first recorded lie in the Bible – uttered by the father of lies:

And the serpent said unto the woman, Ye shall not surely die: For God doth know that in the day ye eat thereof, then your eyes

22

shall be opened, and ye shall be as gods, knowing good and evil. (Gen. 3:4-5)

The first recorded lie is an attack on God Himself as LIFE — as the only source of life. Satan was telling Eve that it was possible for them to possess life within themselves as their own; it was possible for them to possess Truth within themselves as their own. They did not need to abide in God. They could have it all within themselves.

Can we see that this is a repeat of the sin of Satan himself? Sure. And once Adam made the choice to sin, on the human level, the same sin that Satan had committed on the angelic level, there was established IN fallen man an access point for Satan — a fallen human nature that had a correspondence to the fallen angelic nature.

So we see that eating of the forbidden tree — the choice to do so — was really a choice that Adam made to have life in himself. It was a declaration of independence.

Now, if you go back to God's commands, you will notice that God did not say that if Adam ate of the forbidden tree that God would become so angry that He would punish Adam with death. No. Rather, God said that if Adam ate of the forbidden tree, "you will surely die." The point is, the WAGES of sin is death. When Adam chose to walk away from LIFE he died. Sure. God IS life. Reject Him and you will die.

What we see in this is a universal reality. God is sovereign. He is the ONLY source of LIFE and

LIGHT. There is no corner of all creation that is not subject to this fact. In other words, built into the very fabric of God's creation is relationship to Himself. If any being rejects God, who is LIFE and LIGHT, the result is DEATH and DARKNESS. It is the just judgment of God that this be so – if God is God there is no other possibility.

This must be understood lest we think that the death of Adam was arbitrary, or that it was simply God's punishment for sin. No. The death of Adam was perfect justice because the sin of Adam was the rejection of God Himself. The judgment of God is not based on some arbitrary decision that God makes, or upon some temper tantrum that God has towards sin. The judgment of God is based upon His very nature and character. If we sin against God the result MUST be death – because God is God; if God is holy; if God is just.

The enormity of Adam's sin – the deliberate conscious choice to reject God – the depth of evil in this sin is seen in the consequences that followed. Adam not only died spiritually, but his body began to die. And he plunged the entire human race into the realm of death and darkness. We can hardly imagine the heights from which Adam fell – until we begin to catch a glimpse of redemption through Jesus Christ.

"You shall not surely die." That was the lie of Satan. And today it continues to be the lie of Satan. It is just worded a little differently. Today, Satan says, "You need not die." This is a denial of the Cross. It is a denial that humanity MUST die in Christ Jesus in order to be raised in

Him.   Such a denial is everywhere today even within the visible church.

The Aftermath of Adam's Sin

God's original mind for humanity was that the human race be, "naked and ashamed."   Note again that God created humanity to be limited and dependent upon HIM.   But after the sin, we see a terrible change in Adam.   He was no longer, "naked and unashamed" – but he was, "naked and ashamed" – indeed, he was tormented and fearful, "because he was naked."

And the eyes of them both were opened, and they knew that they* [were] *naked; and they sewed fig leaves together, and made themselves aprons. And they heard the voice of the LORD God walking in the garden in the cool of the day: and Adam and his wife hid themselves from the presence of the LORD God amongst the trees of the garden. (Gen. 3:7-8)

Notice that Adam was naked both BEFORE the sin, and AFTER the sin. Of course, the human race is evermore naked – and always will be. But the change from being unashamed to being ashamed and fearful was because Adam was no longer one with God. In other words, he was utterly barren – but God was no longer his source for ALL.

Adam and Eve reacted to the consequences of their sin against God by trying to FIX what they had done to themselves. It says they hid from God -- and they sewed fig leaves to cover themselves.   In other words, they were so

25

distraught over their condition that they tried to cover it – and since there were no other human being around, it is clear they were trying to hide themselves from God.

Human beings have been doing the same ever since – trying to fix ourselves and hide from God. We also sew fig leaves – we do whatever we can to try to cover our true condition. One of the most common, "fig leaves," we use is religion – a religion that we think will cover us with self-righteousness. This is always deception. We are naked and God sees it.

Now, what happens next in the Genesis account is revealing. Ask: Adam sinned the greatest sin against God that any human being ever sinned. But in the aftermath of that sin, WHO came looking for WHO? Adam did not seek God. Rather, God came seeking out Adam. And in that we find the first promise of a REDEEMER.

And I will put enmity between thee (Satan) and the woman, and between thy seed and her seed; it shall bruise thy head, and thou shall bruise his heel..... Unto Adam also and to his wife did the LORD God make coats of skins, and clothed them. (Gen. 3:14-15, 21)

Within this account we see God's true attitude towards the sinner. HE seeks out the sinner for the purpose of Redemption.

This is the first promise of a Redeemer who would be born into the human race – the SEED. And you will note that immediately God introduces the

26

need for a sacrifice who would die in the place of Adam.

Herein we see a great Truth: God CANNOT simply wave His hand and excuse sin. He cannot simply, "make sin go away," or, "make the consequences for sin go away." We have already seen why: God is life and light. To simply save His hand and ignore sin would mean that God would need to deny Himself, and deny the purpose for which He created humanity. If sin does not result in death, then God is not life – God is not God. He would be sanctioning sin against Himself. Divine justice would be negated.

What this means is that God CANNOT forgive sin unless He has a just and moral reason for doing so. The fact that redemption required the life of God's Son proves that God cannot just wave His hand and undo sin. He had to redeem the sinner with a sacrifice that would serve to satisfy eternal justice and holiness.

Justice Satisfied in Christ

Adam sinned, and thus, Adam must die. There is nothing that can lift that penalty for sin. When Jesus died, the penalty for sin was not lifted. Rather, it was satisfied.

The death of Jesus was the death of the Adam race. God's justice was satisfied. But through the resurrection of Christ was the ushering in of a NEW race: The new creation in Christ Jesus.

The NT clearly depicts that this is exactly what Jesus did for humanity:

27

For [there is] one God, and one mediator between God and men, the man Christ Jesus; Who gave himself a ransom for all, to be testified in due time. (I Tim. 2:5-6)

Even as the Son of man came not to be ministered unto, but to minister, and to give his life a ransom for many. (Matt. 20:28)

For ye are bought with a price. (I Cor. 6:20)

God originally created Adam to be one with Himself, and to have, from out of that relationship with God -- to have dominion over God's creation. Redemption is unto that end – that GOD might have His will and purpose. And humanity has the privilege of receiving it by God's grace.

Jesus Christ died and was raised so that the human race could die IN HIM and be RAISED in HIM. That is REDEMPTION for the human race. But as we have seen, it is all unto even greater purpose for the eternal ages. God wants a people who will be coheirs with Christ – who can be expressions and extensions of His Son in the eternal ages.

Chapter 4
The Last Adam

And so it is written, The first man Adam was made a living soul; the last Adam was made a quickening spirit. (1 Cor. 15:45)

Now that we have review the creation of, and the sin of, the first man, Adam, we need to look closer at Jesus as The Last Adam; The Son of Man. This Truth is basic to the Redemption.

In first Corinthians 15, Paul draws a contrast between the man God created, the first Adam – and Jesus Christ – Whom Paul calls, "THE LAST ADAM. Of course, the name, "Adam," actually means, "man."

It is important to take note that the first man, Adam, was the only human being that God ever CREATED. Eve was not created in the same way – she was formed from out of Adam. And everyone else who is human was BORN from out of Adam and Eve.

This is an important point because it shows that Adam is the source of the entire human race. God had created Adam in His image and likeness, and it was God's original intention that the human race be multiplied through Adam and Eve,

We saw how God created Adam to be NAKED and UNSHAMED. "Naked," means God created the human race to have NOTHING in themselves of life, or light, or righteousness. But that was good because God intended for the human race to find

29

life in God Himself – which is why Adam could be naked, but nevertheless unashamed. This was God's NORMAL for humanity.

All of that came crashing down. The sin of Adam was not merely that he ate of fruit that God forbade him to eat. That was only the outward. His sin was that he declared independence from God – and chose to find life in himself rather than through God.

We see this pictured by comparing the forbidden tree to the tree of life. In eating of the forbidden tree – the tree of the knowledge of good and evil, Adam decided for himself what was right and wrong. And instead of dependence upon God – Who IS the tree of life – in eating Adam was breaking union with God and choosing life in and out from himself.

This was no mere mistake. It was a deliberate and knowing choice, in the face of all light and Truth, to align himself with the price of evil.

Why did the sin of Adam result in the entire human race falling into the realm of darkness, corrupted with the sin nature?

First of all, it is difficult to grasp what is known as, "the heredity of sin," because we have little frame of reference for the kind of human being God originally created – a human being without the sin nature, who was alive with the spirit of God. But the kind of human being that Adam became once he severed his relationship with God with a different kind of human being than what God created. Without union with God, he had only a natural life — subject to the realm of darkness. Every dimension of Adam's nature was corrupted and ruined — to where his humanity was reduced to a hollow shell of what God originally created.

Adam had ONLY THAT to pass on to his children. That which is born of the flesh IS flesh — we might also say that because Adam was now fully flesh he could birth ONLY flesh. Again — the sin of Adam had severed his union with God. His entire being had become altered — physically, psychically, and spiritually. Sin had corrupted him into a different kind of human being right down to his core.

Adam now carried these dimensions of the corrupted human race -- and they would be passed down through human reproduction just as surely as he passed down physical traits.

This is why God inspired these words:

In Adam all die, but in Christ all are made alive. (I Cor. 15:22)

What Adam became as a human being is now what humanity IS. There is no escape from what humanity IS — and of course, that leads to what humanity does. In short, all of humanity is the collective ADAM. Humanity is out from Adam because all of humanity is IN ADAM — and that leaves humanity in death.

Everyone who is born of Adam carries the corrupt nature of Adam. It simply takes different forms, and manifests in a variety of ways. It is worked out through works, thinking, and evil. The Bible refers to the nature of Adam as, "the body of sin," "the old man," "the flesh," "the psyche nature," or, "the natural man," in its corrupt condition. But in the final analysis, the Adam nature is SELF as severed from God. It is what a human being is without God – a dead spirit ruled over by the soul realm, in a physical body – subject to the realm of darkness.

The Last Adam

In Adam all die, but in Christ all are made alive. (I Cor. 15:22)

And so it is written, The first man Adam was made a living soul; the last Adam was made a quickening spirit. (1 Cor. 15:45)

Here we see TWO men – each representing a kind of human being – and each being the SOURCE out from which others are born. Adam is the head of the original human race – which became corrupt and subject to the realm of darkness. Jesus Christ is the Head of the NEW creation – the new human race – that is born from above.

Jesus Christ is not only called, "The Last Adam," but He is likewise called, "The Son of Man." Indeed, Jesus referred to Himself as, "The Son of Man," more than by any other name. What does that name mean?

Well, as noted, every human being who has ever been born, or ever will be born, is born IN ADAM – is of the Adam race. And all who are born in

Adam are utterly void of life of God. That is why Jesus said:

That which is born of the flesh is flesh; and that which is born of the Spirit is spirit. (John 3:6)

All who are born IN ADAM are, "born of the flesh," and are therefore, as to nature, FLESH. "Flesh," is the SELF principle. Those who are born of the flesh have themselves – they have the independence from God that Adam choose. That is why, "in Adam all die."

Now, Jesus called Himself, "The Son of Man," to continually emphasize the fact that He was God become human. And yes, Jesus Christ was born as a member of the Adam race. Absolutely. The gospels trace his ancestry back to Adam. This is not only without dispute, but it is essential for the salvation of the human race.

Notice: Jesus was born as a member of the Adam race, but He was born INTO the Adam race **_from the outside_**. Jesus had been God the Son from eternity. He is the only human being who ever existed before human birth. Thus, at physical birth, He had a human mother, but God had been His Father from all eternity. He was born the God-man. Jesus did not become someone else at birth – He was the same Person, the Son of God – but now He had taken on the nature of humanity. Yet, because of this, He did not inherit the corrupt sin nature from Adam. He continued to carry the Divine nature, howbeit, along side of his sinless human nature.

So, we see that despite being God BECOME man, Christ was born into the *same* human race that started with Adam. Christ, through His physical birth, was NOT what Adam became through sin, but was the kind of human being that God originally created when He created Adam. He had no sin nature and walked sinless His entire life.

Jesus Christ the Savior

Jesus Christ came to save the Adam race. What does that mean? And how did He do that?

Unfortunately, some folks think that Jesus died to save us from the wrath of His Father. They think that on the Cross Jesus bore the punishment of God — so that God could lift that punishment of death from us and allow us to live. But there is no such thought in the Bible. To find the Truth we need only revisit the Genesis account.

God had warned Adam, "In the day you eat of the forbidden tree you shall surely die." But Adam ate — and he did die spiritually. He also did eventually die physically. Adam's fate is the unchangeable fate of the entire human race. But Jesus became a member of the Adam race for the purpose of offering Himself as a substitute for us as THE ADAM who must die. Jesus became, "the Adam," who died for the Adam race.

But there is more. Jesus died as our substitute. But what that really means is that Jesus BORE US on the Cross. On the Cross, The Last Adam bore in His body the entire Adam race. This made it possible for us, by faith, to die IN HIM.

Here we see the meaning of Jesus as, "the Last Adam." Jesus was the LAST Adam in that He was the fullness of Adam – the fullness of what God wanted humanity to become. He was the LAST Adam because in filling up God's will for humanity there was no need for another. God's will was fully accomplished in the Son of Man.

But Jesus was likewise the Last Adam because He laid down his perfected, human life for us all. But He did more than simply offer God a legal satisfaction for sin – He did more than just bear the judgment of God for sin. He did that. But on the Cross, Jesus bore SIN itself – indeed, Jesus bore the Adam race on the Cross. And then He died. In short, the Adam race died in Christ – the Adam race ended in Christ. The entire Adam race was gathered up and placed in Christ on the Cross and brought to an end. That is why Jesus is THE Last Adam.

Thus, the death that God pronounced upon Adam because of sin was never lifted because of Christ – rather, it was fully met in Christ. Adam died in Christ. The Adam race was finished when the Christ died.

This is proven by the fact that through the resurrection of Christ we never find any suggestion of a, "fixed up Adam race." No. We find a brand new race – a new creation in Christ. The new creation IS new because the old Adam race is finished. Indeed, unless the Adam race was finished at the Cross, there can be no new creation in Christ Jesus.

The Son of Man

Jesus Christ did not simply make a new creation. He IS the new creation. That is why He is called, "the firstborn of many brethren." We are not new creations separate from Christ. Rather, we are new creations IN CHRIST. Only if we are joined to Him in resurrection union — alive with HIS LIFE — are we new creations.

None of that would be possible unless, "the Word was made flesh" — lived a sinless life, died, and was raised, and ascended AS A HUMAN BEING; as the LAST ADAM. Everything God has for human being was made possible because Jesus Christ became a human being.

The Son of God became a human being so that human beings could become one with God in Him. In Christ, human beings are given ALL that God has to give. In Christ, human beings can inherit all that Jesus Christ has inherited.

Chapter 5
The Gospel of Redemption in Christ

The gospel -- the good news -- is not merely a message about the historical acts of redemption finished by Jesus. Obviously, those are included in the gospel – for without those redemptive acts we could not be saved. But the gospel is the proclamation, and the revelation, of a PERSON: Christ Jesus.

Christ in you, the hope of glory: <u>WHOM</u> we preach. (I Cor. 1:27-28)

To put it another way: The gospel is not only the message of the Cross – it is the revelation of the One Who hung on it – and the revelation that we can die in Him. The gospel is not only the message of the resurrection – it is the revelation of the One who was raised for us – and the revelation that we can be raised in Him. The gospel is not only the message of the ascension – it is the revelation of the One who is seated at the right hand of God – and the revelation that we can be seated in Him.

Gather all of this up and you have Christianity:

CHRIST IN YOU, the hope of glory. (Col 1:27)

He that is joined to the Lord is one spirit with Him. (I Cor. 6:17)

In whom we have redemption. (Col. 1:14)

If we are IN CHRIST – if Christ is IN US; if we are joined to the Lord – then we are made one with the Person IN WHOM is all redemption. All that He DID becomes a living, dynamic reality in us because HE IS IN US – we are ONE WITH HIM.

This cannot be overemphasized. It is the core of Christianity – that Christ not only DID all, but that Jesus Christ IS all -- and the believer is joined to Him. That means that the believer is made one with the ONE IN WHOM is all redemption.

The finished redemptive acts of Jesus Christ – His sinless life, His death on the Cross, His resurrection from the dead, and His ascension – these historical, redemptive acts are the basis for God's entire eternal plan and purpose. But they are all gathered up into, and carried IN A PERSON. Jesus Christ is Christ crucified. Jesus Christ is Christ risen. Jesus Christ is Christ ascended. Eternally, Jesus Christ carries in Himself the fullness of redemption – the fullness of what those historical acts accomplished.

We must never reduce the gospel into a message ABOUT Jesus Christ – or reduce it into a message of only what Jesus Christ did. No. The gospel is the proclamation and revelation of the PERSON – included in whom is all that He did.

Everything that God will ever give to humanity is given IN, and only IN, the Person of His Son. Do we want eternal life? Well, God will not give us a THING called, "eternal life." Rather, God will give us Jesus Christ, the Person – Who is THE LIFE.

38

So again -- we MUST see this: The gospel -- the good news -- is not merely a message about the historical acts of redemption finished by Jesus. But the gospel is the proclamation, and the revelation, of a PERSON: Christ Jesus. IN HIM alone do we have redemption.

For God So Loved

God sent His Son to deliver us all from sin through His death on the Cross -- and He sent Christ to usher in a new creation through His resurrection. But these historical acts have eternal impacts – impacts that remain in the Person of His Son. God sent Christ to die and be raised so that we could be restored back to God IN HIM.

For God so loved the world, that he gave his only begotten Son, that whosoever believes in him should not perish, but have everlasting life. For God sent not his Son into the world to condemn the world; but that the world through him might be saved. (John 3:16-17)

You will note the essential of FAITH. But faith is not merely a matter of believing that the historical acts of Redemption happened. It is not only a matter of believing doctrines. All of these matters will be gathered up in our faith – but faith is more. If we really BELIEVE it means that we will give ourselves to the One we believe. We will relinquish ourselves to Him. – believing that we will be joined to Him in Spirit.

Faith in Christ for salvation means that we relinquish ourselves and fully embrace HIM – we fully embrace being joined to Him in spirit. This ends our life and makes Jesus Christ our life. Christ is then IN US and we are no longer our own. We are saved because we are one in spirit with Life Himself.

How can we know we are saved? In the final analysis, our faith must rest upon HIS FAITHFULNESS. Our faith must not be, "faith in our ability to believe." It must not be even partially in anything about us. Our faith will rest fully upon the One who is faithful. We know we are saved because He said that if we believe we will be saved – and He is faithful that promised.

Repent and Believe

The good news of the gospel states that you and I do not need to do anything to be saved except, "Repent and believe on Christ." That means that we must realize we are lost sinners, and desire to forsake our lives and any sin into the hands of God through Christ. Basically, it means that we cry out to God in need for salvation. It means that we come to the Cross and commit our entire trust for salvation to Jesus Christ and what He has done. As noted, we forsake our life in Adam and fully embrace Christ as our life – in resurrection union with Him.

We must REPENT and BELIEVE. What of what must we repent? UNBELIEF. In other words, we must repent of NOT believing. But if we repent of NOT believing, then what will we do? Well, we will BELIEVE.

40

Unbelief is the sin of which we must repent. Unbelief is a refusal to come to Christ – whether it is through ignorant self-will, neglect, or simply by owning ourselves. All other sins are gathered up in unbelief. Repentance, which is a change of moral mind towards God, is a renunciation of myself and my unbelief, and a turning to Christ by faith. It results in Christ IN US.

If we repent of unbelief it means we will be in communion with the One in Whom there is freedom from sin. It is nonsense to try to overcome SINS unless we repent of THE SIN in which all others are rooted: Unbelief or self-ownership.

By Grace through Faith

We cannot earn salvation, and there is nothing we can do to KEEP saved. In fact, according to the Bible, good works are the outcome of salvation, and not the means of earning it.

For by grace are you saved through faith; and that not of yourselves: it is the gift of God: Not of works, lest any man should boast. For we are his workmanship, created in Christ Jesus unto good works, which God has before ordained that we should walk in them. (Eph 2:8-10)

Salvation is, "by grace though faith," because that is the ONLY way in which God could save us. Jesus did for us what we could never do, but now that He has finished His redemptive work, Jesus Christ IS unto us what we can never be:

But of him are ye in Christ Jesus, who of God is made unto us wisdom, and righteousness, and sanctification, and redemption: That, according as it is written, He that glories, let him glory in the Lord. (I Cor. 1:30-31)

Other Essentials

Jesus Christ was the only begotten Son of God. He left that position in heaven and became a man. Such was the sacrifice He made to even come to this earth. Jesus was God -- the Word of God – the only begotten Son of God – and God gave Him to us. This gift began to unfold when Jesus left the Father, and while remaining God, and was born of a virgin -- became a flesh and blood human being.

Christ Jesus, who existing in nature and character as God, did not consider equality with God a prize to be grasped at and retained for Himself. But He emptied Himself, and took upon himself the state of a servant, and He as God came to be in the likeness of men. (Phil 2:6-10)

And the Word was made flesh, and dwelt among us, (and we beheld his glory, the glory as of the only begotten of the Father,) full of grace and truth. (John 1:14)

The virgin birth was essential because it means that Jesus did not begin to exist when He was conceived in Mary. No. Rather, He preexisted as God -- and was supernaturally transferred into Mary's womb – now as a tiny life. This is what is referred to as, "the Immaculate Conception."

42

This miracle conception made it possible for Him to be born as a human being, yet remain fully as the eternal Son of God. And since Jesus was born of a virgin, and not the product of human reproduction, it means He was not born of the fallen human race. He was born without a sin nature.

When Jesus was born of the virgin Mary into this world, that BEGAN His journey. He lived a perfectly sinless life for over 33 years. The Bible calls Him, "The Lamb of God without blemish."

For we have not an high priest which cannot be touched with the feeling of our infirmities; but was in all points tempted like as we are, yet without sin. (Heb 4:15)

For God has made Jesus to be like sin for us, even though Christ knew no sin; that we might be made the righteousness of God in him. (2 Cor. 5:21)

Death and Resurrection

At the end of His sinless life, and at the end of the three and one-half years of ministry, Jesus offered Himself up to the Cross for us all.

And being seen and known as a man, he humbled himself, and became obedient unto death, even the death of the cross.

Jesus Christ did NOT die for an elect few. Jesus died for every human being that ever has, or ever will, live – and His Redemption paid for every sin that has ever been committed by every human being.   (Except for the sin of refusing Him.) Therefore, God offers Christ to ALL – no matter the sin, and no matter how old they are. "Whoever calls on the name of the Lord will be saved." The good news is that Jesus died for ALL – and God invites all to come to Christ. But only those who do come and believe are saved.

Not only did Jesus win for us the forgiveness of God for all sin, but He also made possible for us to be DELIVERED from all bondage to sin. This is possible because Jesus did die FOR us – and in doing so, made in possible for us – by being planted into His death to die in Him.

I am crucified with Christ: nevertheless I live; yet not I, but Christ liveth in me: and the life which I now live in the flesh I live by the faith of the Son of God, who loved me, and gave himself for me. (Gal 2:20)

Know ye not, that so many of us as were baptized into Jesus Christ were baptized into his death? Therefore we are buried with him by baptism into death: that like as Christ was raised up from the dead by the glory of the Father, even so we also should walk in newness of life. For if we have been planted together in the likeness of his death, we shall be also in the likeness of his resurrection: Knowing this, that our old man is crucified with him, that the body of sin might be destroyed, that henceforth we should not serve sin. For he that is dead is freed from sin. Now if we be dead with Christ, we believe that we shall also live with him: Knowing that Christ being raised from the dead dies no more; death has no more dominion over him. For in that he died, he died unto sin once: but in that he lives, he lives unto God. Likewise reckon you also yourselves to be dead indeed unto sin, but alive unto God through Jesus Christ our Lord. (Rom 6:3-11)

So through His death, Jesus delivered us from the Adam race, and therefore, from the basis of all sin. That is why Jesus told us we must LOSE our lives in order to find Him as our life. Doing so is not an act of faith that is, "extra," to being saved. No. It is nothing more than our giving of ourselves to Christ as our salvation.

Christ in You

But of him are ye in Christ Jesus, who of God is made unto us...redemption. (I Cor. 1:30)

"Christ in us, the hope of glory" (Col. 1:27) – this is another way of describing a believer joined to the Lord and made one spirit with Him. But can we see in this is that Jesus Christ IS our redemption? If we are joined to Him in spirit we are redeemed. If we are not joined to Him, we are not redeemed. If we are joined to Him, we are alive with His life. If we are not joined to Him, we are dead in our life. If we are joined to Him we are raised in Him and He IS our salvation; He is our life.

This is why, "Christ in you, the hope of glory" (Col. 1:27), is really a description of Christianity. Christ is ALL, and ALL is given in Christ. He IS all to the believer. And ALL that God is doing is OUT FROM HIM and BUILT upon Him.

The Sin-Bearer

In whom we have redemption. (Eph. 1:7)

Who his own self bare our sins in his own body on the tree, that we, being dead to sins, should live unto righteousness: by whose stripes ye were healed. (1 Pet 2:24)

Behold the Lamb of God, which takes away the sin of the world. (John 1:29)

On the Cross, Jesus bore the entirety of the Adam race in Himself and brought that Adam race down to death. Thus, the death of Christ did not appease God so that death could be lifted from us. Rather, the death of Christ fully satisfied the justice and judgment of God for sin – and made it possible for us to die IN HIM – thus, being set free from the old creation. Jesus became sin for us – Jesus became us; Jesus became Adam – by bearing ALL in Himself. That ended the Adam race. Then, through the resurrection, Jesus ushered in a NEW humanity – a new creation in Himself.

You will note that Jesus Christ died – as The Last Adam – for the ENTIRE Adam race. Indeed, the entire Adam race died in Him. That is every human being to ever be born or who will ever be born. No exceptions. But it is ONLY those who believe and come to Christ who will be saved.

Now, if you think about this, it means we are NOT saved solely by the death of Christ on the Cross. No. Death is death. It is only those who put their faith in Christ that, yes, die in Him, but who are saved by His LIFE — saved by being raised in Him as new creations.

For if, when we were enemies, we were reconciled to God by the death of his Son, much more, being reconciled, we shall be saved by his life. (Rom. 5:10)

It would NOT be true that we are saved by His LIFE if the death of Jesus were merely an appeasement of God. For if that were the case, once God was appeased, there would be no need for a new creation; no need for newness of life. But despite the fact that we must take our place in His death — be baptized into His death — it is actually through the resurrection union with Jesus Christ that we are saved.

So what does all of this tell us? It tells us that salvation is not merely a matter of getting a ticket to heaven. Rather, salvation is a matter of the END of my life in Adam, and the beginning of life in Christ. Salvation is the result of being joined to LIFE HIMSELF.

Resurrection Union

When we come to Jesus Christ, and give ourselves to Him, we are joined to Him in resurrection union:

But he that is joined unto the Lord is one spirit. (I Cor. 6:17)

We are made one with Christ IN SPIRIT — but not in physical body or psyche (soul). But because we are joined to the One Who IS LIFE, this means that we are ALIVE with HIS LIFE. That is salvation. Thus, salvation or eternal life is not a THING or merely a legal classification that God give us. No. God gives us CHRIST HIMSELF — who then becomes our life through resurrection union.

For if we have been planted together in the likeness of his death, we shall be also [in the likeness] of [his] resurrection: (Rom. 6:5)

Baptism INTO Christ is equal to being joined to Him in one spirit. The entire Adam race was planted into Christ on the Cross. But only those who take their place in His death by faith — relinquish themselves to Christ through repentance — are raised with Him. That is salvation. It is resurrection life in Christ. It is oneness with Him in HIS LIFE.

Preaching the Person

The good news is the proclamation and the revelation of the Person, Jesus Christ. It includes all of His redemptive acts — but also includes the Person of Jesus Christ RIGHT NOW. Human beings are invited to, "repent and believe" — for all that God has done, and has given, and all that God will ever give, is bound up in the Person of His Son.

Chapter 6
The Finished Work of Jesus Christ

In this chapter we want to look at some of the questions, issues, and terms having to do with the Redemption.

There is therefore no condemnation for those who are in Christ Jesus. (Romans 8:1)

Condemnation is never of God for those who are in Christ. Why? Because Christ has already bore all sin — bore the Adam race — down into death, thus satisfying all justice and judgment. Furthermore, if we are in Christ, then we are one in spirit with Him — we are in resurrection union with Him. How can we be under condemnation if we are IN CHRIST?

Paul declares outright, "There is NO condemnation for those in Christ." So in light of His declaration, let's ask these questions:

Is there NO condemnation for those in Christ **EXCEPT** when we sin?

OR

Is there NO condemnation for those in Christ **EVEN** when we sin?

Well, if there is NO condemnation for those in Christ **EXCEPT** when we sin, then there IS condemnation for those in Christ **when** we sin. Right? When else would there be condemnation if not **when** we sin?

49

But if there is NO condemnation for those in Christ **EVEN** when we sin, then there is **never** condemnation for those in Christ – for when else would condemnation apply if not when we sin?

Clearly, this Truth emerges: There is never condemnation for those in Christ **EVEN** when we sin. None.

Grace Always Abounds

There is another verse about which we can have a similar discussion:

> *Shall we continue in sin, that grace may abound? (Rom. 6:1)*

Ask: Does grace abound **EXCEPT** when we sin?

OR

Does grace abound **EVEN** when we sin?

Well, if grace abounds **EXCEPT** when we sin, then grace does not abound at all, does it? – for when we sin is when we need grace to abound the most.

But if grace abounds **EVEN** when we sin, then it always abounds because it is finished in Christ – and believers are IN HIM.

All Things Are Out From Christ

> *Therefore if any man [be] in Christ, [he is] a new creature: old things are passed away; behold, all things are become new. And all*

things [are] of God, who hath reconciled us to himself by Jesus Christ, and hath given to us the ministry of reconciliation; To wit, that God was in Christ, reconciling the world unto himself, not imputing their trespasses unto them; and hath committed unto us the word of reconciliation. Now then we are ambassadors for Christ, as though God did beseech [you] by us: we pray [you] in Christ's stead, be ye reconciled to God. For he hath made him [to be] sin for us, who knew no sin; that we might be made the righteousness of God in him. (II Cor. 5:17-21)

The above passage can certainly be considered a summary of the gospel; a summary of the finished work of Jesus Christ – and what that means for humanity. And yet the good news contained in this passage is often either overlooked, or corrupted, by religious flesh. That is why it merits a close examination.

Paul begins by stating the Truth we are seeing over and over again: Christian person is one who is IN CHRIST. Or, if you prefer, a Christian person is one in whom Christ dwells. (Col. 1:27) This corresponds to his words to this same Corinthian church in his first letter – it is there that Paul tells us HOW Christ dwells in the believer:

He that is joined to the Lord is one spirit (with Him). (I Cor. 6:17)

Here we again see that the believers are one in spirit with the risen Christ. That is why He is our life; why we are alive with His life — in other words, saved.

Paul tells us that this resurrection, spiritual union with Christ constitutes the NEW CREATION in Christ. Note that the believer is not, "acted upon," and morphed INTO a new creation simply because of faith in Christ. Neither is a person a new creation only in a legal sense. No. The believer BECOMES -- and IS -- a new creation solely because of spiritual union WITH Christ: "If anyone is IN CHRIST they ARE a new creation." This is, of course, equal to the NEW BIRTH.

Now, what follows in Paul's description of what it means to be IN CHRIST is essential to see. But there is a translation problem here. The KJV and many other versions read, "old things are passed away." That is not correct. The Greek actually reads, "old things are passed BY; old things are passed OVER." What does that mean?

Well, first, what are these, "old things?" Well, if we are joined to the Lord and made one spirit with Him — if that is what it means to be IN CHRIST — if that spiritual union constitutes the new creation — then the old things that are passed over must be all that is NOT united with Christ; not in Him. And what would those things be? Not our human spirit — for that IS united with Christ. No. What is not united with Christ is our physical body and our natural, soul man. These are NOT united with Christ in spirit — they could not be, for they are NOT spirit. Rather, they remain outside of our spiritual union with Christ — they are passed over

– that is -- not incorporated into the new creation in Christ Jesus.

It ought to make sense that Paul would say that our physical body and natural soul man are PASSED OVER as it pertains to the new creation -- rather than passed AWAY. Our physical bodies and natural soul man haven't passed away – and don't we know that! We deal with them every day.

So, what Paul is describing here is what is often referred to as, "the separation of soul from spirit," in the believer. When the believer puts faith in Christ, it is then that Christ joins us to Himself in spirit – our human spirit united with Him by the means of the Holy Spirit – and we become a new creation IN HIM. That is the new man; the inner man. But our physical body and natural soul man are NOT united with Him in this age. They remain outside of this resurrection union. Thus, we have a separation between that which IS united with Christ – the spirit – and that which is NOT united with Christ – the natural. The Bible often refers to this distinction as, "the flesh vs. the spirit."

Having established that separation – having defined what constitutes the new creation in Christ Jesus – Paul then makes this statement: "All things are become new -- and all things are OUT FROM God." This is the Greek reading.

What is Paul referring to when he says, "All things are become new?" Well, we have already seen that the OLD things that are passed over with regards to the new creation are the physical body and natural soul man – these remain outside of our resurrection union with Christ. Therefore, what Paul is referring to when he says, "all things are become new," is the new creation. The union of a human being with Jesus Christ -- by the spirit of God -- births a NEW creation; a NEW man. All that emerges in this birth is brand NEW – that is – is did not exist in the Adam race. It exists only because of resurrection union with Jesus Christ.

What Paul says next verifies all of this. The verse division between verses 17 and 18 is unfortunate because it tends to cloud Paul's thought. He is actually saying, "All things that are of the new creation in Christ are OUT FROM GOD – but no things that are of the new creation in Christ are out from the natural man -- for natural man is passed over as it pertains to the new creation."

"All things are out from God." In other words, WE bring no value to resurrection union. Jesus Christ is the value – and we are recipients. ALL that is eternal, holy, and of value in the new creation is OUT FROM the Person of Jesus Christ.

This is so essential to grasp. There is absolutely NO contribution to the new creation in Christ Jesus that comes from our old nature; from our natural man. No. That is passed by; passed over -- nothing that is of God in our lives is OUT FROM ourselves. But ALL that is of God in the life of the believer – ALL that is new is OUT FROM God through the Christ with Whom we are joined in spirit. ALL is out from Christ – NOTHING is out from us. That is a complete separation; a complete setting aside of natural man and shows that Jesus Christ is the very life of the believer.

This also shows the danger of incorporating into the spiritual life that which God says is passed over – the natural man. No. There is nothing that can be found in natural man – not even what we might call "good" – that has been incorporated by God into the new creation. Thus, if WE incorporate any part of natural man into the new creation we are in error. We are bringing in corruption.

The way in which God deals with this issue is by bringing the believer under the work of the Cross so that the natural man might be experientially crucified – in order that Christ, who is our life, might be manifested. All of this is already a done deal. But because humanity has a free will, and because God wants us to grow to KNOW HIM – it all must be worked out and experienced. Paul is simply giving us the Truth.

Reconciliation

This great Truth of the new creation in Christ – and what that really means – is preliminary to the statements that follow in this passage by the apostle Paul. They are statements that are so wonderful, freeing, and eternal, that they have often been buried under the corruption of religious flesh. Let's read them again:

And all things are OUT FROM God, who hath reconciled us to himself by Jesus Christ, and hath given to us the ministry of reconciliation; To wit, that God was in

***Christic, reconciling the world unto himself,
not imputing their trespasses unto them;
and hath committed unto us the word of
reconciliation.***

The first thing we notice in this passage is that
God has reconciled US to HIMSELF – by Jesus
Christ. There is no suggestion in all of scripture
that God ever needed to be reconciled back to
humanity. No. The problem between God and
humanity has always been humanity. And that
problem has never been limited to what we
DO. The problem is what we ARE. The Adam
race is a dead race; utterly and completely at
enmity against God. This is why the redemption
of the Adam race was MORE than a matter of
forgiveness for sins. Rather, redemption for the
Adam race required a full deliverance from what
we are through death and resurrection unto a new
creation in Christ Jesus.

The fact that humanity had to be reconciled back
to God is seen in the garden story. Adam HID
from God. God came seeking out Adam. Indeed,
God initiated reconciliation by slaying an animal
and giving the first promise of a Redeemer.

All Are Reconciled Back to God

What Paul states next in this passage is not
commonly understood or preached. Religious
tradition and self-righteousness has blinded most
of us to the enormity of the Truth that Paul
states. He says:

***God, who hath reconciled us to himself by
Jesus Christ, and hath given to us the***

56

ministry of reconciliation; To wit, that God was in Christ, reconciling the world unto himself, not imputing their trespasses unto them; and hath committed unto us the word of reconciliation.

Note two phrases in this passage: First, "God HAS (past tense) reconciled us to Himself by Jesus Christ." Second, "God was in Christ (past tense) reconciling the world unto Himself — NOT IMPUTING their trespasses unto them." You have TWO groups being spoken of — "US," meaning believers, and, "the world," meaning unbelievers. Yet Paul states that God has already reconciled both US and THE WORLD to Himself through Jesus Christ. Indeed, he even states that because God has reconciled the world to Himself, He is NOT IMPUTING their sins unto them. That is astounding. But what does that really mean?

It means that full reconciliation is a completed work for every human being that has ever lived or will live. It means the unbelievers are just as much reconciled to God as are believers. Read it. That is what it says. And just so we would not misunderstand, Paul says that God is, "not imputing," the sins of unbelievers unto them — precisely because of the reconciliation that Christ has finished for them.

Yet how many of us actually believe that? Most of us do not believe it. What we believe is that believers are reconciled to God because we believe — and that unbelievers are not reconciled to God because they don't believe. Yet Paul is clearly stating that ALL are reconciled to God whether they believe or not — God is not imputing sin even to unbelievers.

Is this universal salvation? Is Paul saying that people are saved whether they believe or not? NO. We need to be clear about that. Paul is NOT saying all are saved whether they believe or not — He is not saying that all are in Christ as new creations whether they believe or not. He is simply saying that all are reconciled back to God whether they believe it or know it. Being reconciled to God is not equal to salvation. Being reconciled to God simply means that Jesus Christ has removed all obstacles between God and humanity — by taking away the sin of humanity — by no longer imputing sin to humanity. This does not mean that everyone will actually believe or embrace that great Truth.

And therein is the entire issue. Jesus Christ has — in Himself -- reconciled the entire human race back to God. He has taken away all sin — taken away every sin that could separate humanity from God. But we must put our faith in Christ for it to do us any good. We must come to Christ by faith and enter into the reconciliation Christ has wrought. Otherwise, we cannot be saved.

Salvation is offered to all — but only in Christ. Consequently, only those who come to Christ and become those who are IN CHRIST can find the salvation that is only IN CHRIST. We need only believe and embrace Him — knowing this is finished. We need only take our place -- through repentance -- in His death — the death that made this possible. And if we do, and ONLY if we do, will we be raised in Him as new creatures unto newness of life.

To put is simply, the way into the holy of holies is clear for all humanity – the veil is forever rent. There is no sin that you and I could commit that can sew that veil back up and keep us out – there is no sin that can undo what Jesus has done. Therefore, THE ONLY SIN can keep us from entering into the Holy of Holies is the sin of refusing to enter into the Holy of Holies. In other words, THE SIN of unbelief. The only sin that can keep you and I from Jesus Christ is THE SIN of refusing Jesus Christ. THE SIN of refusing Jesus Christ is THE SIN of refusing reconciliation back to God.

Herein we see the ONE sin that has no forgiveness. Jesus Christ died for every sin ever committed by every human being. But He could not die for THE SIN of refusing His death. How could He? That would be a contradiction. Jesus did not die for the sin of refusing His death. God cannot forgive the refusal of His forgiveness. That is why it is the sin that has no forgiveness.

This sin that has no forgiveness is the sin of unbelief – not a temporary lapse of faith – but the sin of finally neglecting or refusing God's only way through Jesus Christ.

You will remember that the first words of the gospel are, "Repent and believe." Well, what do we repent of? Sins? Ok. But ultimately we are to repent of UNBELIEF – and if we do, then we will do what? – we will BELIEVE. And if we do believe then it is only because we have repented of unbelief. Thus, the real issue between God and humanity is not acts of sin. The real issue is faith verses unbelief. If I believe and embrace Christ the sin issue is addressed – all of my other sins come under His Blood. But if I refuse to believe and embrace Christ, then I am refusing to believe that the sin issue is addressed – and am guilty of the ultimate sin of refusing God's deliverance from sin through His Son.

Jesus Christ has reconciled all of humanity back to God. The choice of humanity is whether we will enter BY FAITH into all that His reconciliation has made possible – the choice is faith or unbelief. In short, Jesus died for the entire Adam race. But only those who believe will be united with Christ in resurrection union, and thus saved.

Forgiveness is Finished

And be ye kind one to another, tenderhearted, forgiving one another, even as God for Christ's sake HAS forgiven you. (Eph. 4:32)

And you, being dead in your sins and the uncircumcision of your flesh, HAS he quickened together with Him, HAVING forgiven ALL your trespasses. (Col. 2:13)

I write unto you, little children, because your sins ARE forgiven you for His name's sake. (I John 2:12)

To wit, that God was, in Christ, reconciling the world unto Himself, not imputing their trespasses unto them. (II Cor. 5:19)

"In whom we have redemption through His blood, the forgiveness of sins, according to the riches of His grace." (Eph. 1:7)

The FULL and FINISHED forgiveness of God of humanity is just as FULL and FINISHED as the death of Jesus that made it possible. Jesus died ONCE FOR ALL. That means forgiveness is ONCE FOR ALL. Any other teaching is error.

And yet we have this passage from I John 1:

If we confess our sins, he is faithful and just to forgive us [our] sins, and to cleanse us from all unrighteousness. If we say that we have not sinned, we make him a liar, and his word is not in us. (I John 1:9-10)

It has often been taught from this passage that God only forgives us IF we confess our sins. After all, it is reasoned, if God forgave us even though we do not confess sin, it would be a sanction of sin. Yet that entire line of reasoning is not only contrary to the finished work of Christ, but it is actually contrary to this passage in I John.

If God only forgave confessed sin, how about all of the sins of which we are unaware? And what if we are killed before we confess some sins? Do we die in an unforgiven condition? For that matter, is there such a thing as an, "unforgiven saved person?" Isn't that term a contradiction?

61

The issue here is resolved once we look at the NT Greek. The tense is not translated correctly in most versions. The tense of, "to forgive our sins," ought to be the tense that denotes a past completed act with present results. That perfectly represents the forgiveness of Christ for sin. The verse is best translated, "If we confess our sins, He is faithful and just to have forgiven our sins." Or, we could say, "He is faith and just to be forgiving our sins." Either way, this verse does not say that God forgives us only IF we confess sin, or that God only forgives us AS we confess. It is saying that our sins are already forgiven.

This defines CONFESSION. "Confession," in Greek, means, "to say the same thing." So to confess sin means to say the same thing about it as God says about it. It means to speak the Truth about my sin – it IS sin, I am guilty, but God has fully forgiven it in Christ. In short, I do not confess sin TO GET forgiven. Rather, I confess sin because I am forgiven. My confession is simply a way of putting my faith in His finished work and declaring the Truth.

What we see in all of these matters is that Jesus Christ has done everything there is to do in order to save humanity. And today, Jesus Christ IS the fullness of His finished work – and the fullness of God. That is the gospel. It is the proclamation and revelation of the PERSON – and all that He has done.

Chapter 7
The Essential of Faith

Faith is essential if we are to walk with Jesus Christ. It fact, in Hebrews, we read:

But without faith [it is] impossible to please [him]: for he that cometh to God must believe that he is, and [that] he is a rewarder of them that diligently seek him. (Heb. 11:6)

The Greek text actually reads, "APART from faith it is impossible to please Him." In other words, nothing a person does is of any value if that person is doing it APART – separate from – faith. Thus, all that a person does must be from out of, and the result of, faith in God.

So, we need to ask, "What is faith?"

Faith is never a thing unto itself. Indeed, faith isn't a THING at all. Neither is faith a FORCE that a believer receives from, or generates up to God. Faith is a RELATIONSHIP. All faith is toward God Himself – faith is in the Person of Jesus Christ.

This means that, yes, we believe everything that God has said. But more than that, we believe that God is FAITHFUL and TRUE. When everything is said and done, faith is a rest upon the character of God.

For example, how do you know you are saved? Many Calvinists will tell you that you can know you are saved – you can know that you are one of the elect — by looking at yourself for evidence. Do you love God? Do you desire His Son? Well, they will say, that proves you are saved — it proves you have been regenerated through election. But this is error — because you could be self-deceived.

So how do you know you are saved? There is only one way: By believing Jesus Christ — by believing that HE is faithful and true. Jesus said, "Believe on Me and you will be saved." Believe — and then trust that HE is faithful Who has promised.

Can we see that this puts the entire issue of faith on whether GOD is faithful? That this puts assurance of salvation, not upon any evidence we think we see in ourselves, but upon the faithfulness and trueness of God Himself?

This illustrates the nature of faith. Faith is NOT trust in my faith. Faith is not trust in my discernment of myself. No. Faith is simply trust that God is faithful.

How Faith Comes to Be

So then faith comes by hearing and hearing by the word of God." (Rom. 10:17)

How does a person come to, "have faith," in God? Romans 10:17, above, tells us. But let's notice a couple of things about this verse. First of all, when Paul says that, "faith comes," what is he talking about? He's talking about faith coming TO BE -- IN you and in me. Faith is not, "out there," hanging in the air. Faith comes to be IN people. Faith is a relationship. So when he talks about, "faith coming to be," he is talking about faith coming to be IN US.

But also notice the phrase: "…so then faith COMES". How many see that this very small phrase tells us point blank -- that faith MUST COME. In other words, faith is not in you and I to begin with. No. Paul says, "So then faith COMES" – this is proof that it has to COME. Faith has to come TO BE in you and I -- it is not there to begin with.

Now, that opens up another important Truth. If faith needs to come to BE in you and I -- can we see that this means that true faith does not originate from you and I as the source? Can we see that we are wasting our time trying to, "muster up," faith from out from ourselves? There is no faith in us, by nature, to, "muster up."

There is no faith born into the Adamic race. When you and I were born into this world, we did not have any life in us, nor Truth, and therefore, we did not have any faith in us. It is absolutely impossible for a human being -- left to himself in Adam -- to produce any faith at all unto God. Period.

Now you CAN have human faith – you CAN have religious faith. You can create out of your human imagination a religion -- even a version of Christianity. You can create a (false) CHRIST out of your imagination and think that this is the one who is in you -- and you can put your human faith in that and think this is real faith. People do this kind of thing all the time. But it is not real. It is of human origin -- and true faith is NEVER of human origin.

True faith has to COME TO BE in you and I, which means that the source of true faith has to be from One OTHER THAN OURSELVES -- namely, Jesus Christ. Faith has to come to be -- from the outside of us -- into the inside of us from the outside. Of course it does. This is how Jesus needs to come. I don't know how many times God has to tell us, and to repeat this over and over again, that no one has anything of value except that which is received from ABOVE. (see John 3:27)

So faith has to come to be in you and I. Now, how does it come to be in you and I? Well, Romans 10:17 tells us: Faith comes to be in us by hearing -- and more specifically -- by hearing the Word of God.

We cannot take the time here to refer back to the opening chapter of this book. God is speaking Christ. HE is the Living Word of God. Thus, rather than focus on THINGS we say God is speaking, we need to realize that when all is said and done that God is speaking and revealing a PERSON.

Now notice: Faith comes by HEARING – but HEARING demands that someone is speaking – or else there would be nothing TO hear. In other words, I cannot believe unless God speaks. That is what Romans 10:17 is saying: Faith comes by hearing the Word of God.

God Almighty has to take the initiative to reveal to us Truth; to reveal to us Christ. It is only if He does this -- which we may refer to as speaking or revealing Jesus Christ to us — it is only then that we can HEAR — for only then is there anything TO hear. Then, IF we hear, faith is born.

Faith is a relationship. It is the relationship with God of faith -- and as I have noted -- this is initiated by God when He brings light, or when He speaks and reveals the Truth about Himself. Now if -- and this is a big IF -- we embrace the light and Truth which God brings, then the reality of faith will come TO BE IN US individually.

Truth Makes Hearing Possible

Now, someone is going to ask the, "chicken or egg," question -- "If faith comes by hearing the Word of God, then how do you get enough faith to hear the Word of God?"

Notice that Romans 10:17 does NOT say that initially you must have faith to hear the Word of God. Romans 10:17 says that faith COMES BY HEARING the Word of God. So, the correct order is this: God reveals, we hear, and faith comes to be.

So, the question really is this, "How can a person who has no faith HEAR God? The answer is found, not in the one who needs to hear, but in the One who is speaking. When God speaks it awakens a person — the spirit of God makes us to know enough to turn and hear. When God speaks to you and to me, it can penetrate any blindness, any deafness, or any darkness. God's voice can open ears and eyes.

But God is not going to violate free will. How many notice that in the Bible, God never makes anyone think or do anything? It simply says that God brings light -- and that light will make it possible for us to see and to hear. It does not force us to embrace the Truth or to believe God.

Substance and Evidence

Faith is the substance of things hoped for, and evidence of things not seen. (Heb. 11:1)

We have seen that, "faith comes by hearing the Word of God." Then the above verse adds that real faith IS substance or evidence. But substance and evidence of what? Well, if faith COMES by hearing what God reveals, then this same faith is substance and evidence of what God reveals. In other words, the faith that comes to be in you and I is – spiritually – the substance and evidence IN US of what God has spoken.

Hebrews is telling us that God works IN US – He reveals and we hear – and faith comes to be in us. But because that faith finds its source in what God has spoken, then it is substance and evidence IN US of what God has revealed.

This brings us to a couple of other conclusions. Number one: you cannot have the faith of Jesus Christ for anything except what HE has faith for -- because it's the faith OF Jesus Christ. Or, to put it another way, if faith comes to be in us because God has spoken, and we have heard, then you can't have faith for anything but the Truth that God has spoken.

So, we can do away with the false teaching that if you want something, all you need to do is confess it, brainwash yourself into thinking that you will receive it, and you will receive it. No, you don't get to initiate these things. Faith does not come by SPEAKING or confessing. Faith comes by hearing what GOD speaks – which puts everything within HIS WILL.

Now, what does all of this tell us? It tells us that we need not waste our energy asking God to give us more faith. He never will. We really need to ask God to speak to us more of Christ; more of the Truth. And then keep our hearts open to HEAR. Do that and faith will come to be in us.

Believing God

Let us hold fast the profession of [our] faith without wavering; (for he [is] faithful that promised.) (Heb. 10:23)

And I saw heaven opened, and behold a white horse; and he that sat upon him [was] called Faithful and True. (Rev. 19:11)

When all is said and done, we must ALL answer the question: Is God faithful and true? But not merely in general – but is God faithful and true to us personally and individually? Does God ALWAYS tell the Truth? Can we absolutely trust and rely upon God to be faithful, keep His Word, and do what is best of us? Can we risk our life on Him?

69

Well, if we do believe all of those wonderful things about God, then we have the beginning of faith. But faith must be tested – it must be proven. Faith must be lived out. Thus, if we believe God -- we are going to act like it. We are going to live accordingly – in both the good times and the bad times. But more than that, if we truly believe God we are going to give ourselves to Him in Christ – unconditionally.

Can we see that true faith will always carry us to abandon ourselves to Jesus Christ? We will lose ourselves to Him – we will learn to REST in the fact that He is faithful.

Faith in Jesus Christ – based on the Truth that God reveals – is initially exercised when we accept Christ as our personal Savior. We believe and know that we are saved because Jesus said so – and He is faithful Who has promised. This is a principle that carries through into all facets of the Christian walk, because Jesus Christ never changes.

Chapter 8
Christ, Our Life

For ye are dead, and your life is hid with Christ in God. When Christ, [who is] our life, shall appear, then shall ye also appear with him in glory. (Col. 3:3-4)

It would seem that the most simple and clear proclamations of Truth in the Bible have been blurred and redefined by religious tradition. The result is a widespread blindness among believers – a blindness to Jesus Christ. This passage is a case in point. Paul clearly states that Jesus Christ IS our life. Yet how often is this preached? And if it is preached, is it preached in Truth? Or is it redefined and made to mean something other than the Truth; something less than the Truth?

Note: Paul does not say that Jesus Christ gives us a THING called, "life." Rather, he says that Jesus Christ IS our life. In fact, the clarity with which Paul proclaims this Truth is amazing. He prefaces his statement by telling us that WE are dead. This shows that we are not made alive by being given a THING called, "life." No. We are given CHRIST HIMSELF. Paul says we are dead, BUT: Christ is our life.

Can we see the distinction between being made alive by being given a THING called, "life," – a distinction between that and being made one with the PERSON who said, "I AM the life?"

71

The Truth is, God does not give us THINGS. God gives us Christ in Whom are ALL things. Primary to this Truth is the fact that God does not give us a THING called, "eternal life." Rather, He gives us Christ who IS THE LIFE – and once Christ dwells in us – He is OUR life. And since WE are dead, that means Jesus Christ is the ONLY LIFE of the believer.

Now, how often have we heard this great Truth? Usually, "eternal life," is spoken of as a THING, or as a, "legal classification," or as a, "ticket to heaven." Sometimes it is spoken of as a THING that is given to us in the spirit of God. But how often has it been taught that Jesus Christ IS the life – the only life of the believer?

This is a vital Truth. Behind the simple statement that Jesus Christ IS the life of the believer is the reality that Jesus Christ is ALL to the believer. Sure. ALL is in LIFE. Sure. For outside of LIFE is what? Well, death. Thus, if Jesus Christ IS the life – if Jesus Christ is our life – then Jesus Christ is our ALL.

The fact is, God has given all that He has to give to humanity IN HIS SON. (see Rom. 8:32) He has given NOTHING outside of Christ. The church MUST see this. The church MUST believe this. The church MUST experience Jesus Christ as our life. But it is a Truth to which the church has been blinded.

We Are Dead

How does a believer receive Christ as our life? Well, by relinquishing OURS. You have to repent of possessing your own life, and take your place in the Cross of Jesus. Then you are raised WITH HIM to newness of life -- you relinquish your life and become one with Him in HIS LIFE.

When the believer comes to Christ by faith, we are, "joined to the Lord and are one spirit with Him." (I Cor. 6:17) We are buried with Him by a spiritual baptism in His death, and raised in Him in a spiritual resurrection union. (Rom. 6:4-5) At that point, we are alive – we are alive because we are one in spirit with LIFE HIMSELF.

Paul clearly stated this to the Galatians:

I am crucified with Christ: nevertheless I live; yet not I, but Christ lives in me: and the life which I now live in the flesh I live by the faith of the Son of God, who loved me, and gave himself for me. (Gal. 2:20)

Christ was crucified and died for ALL of us. He was raised for ALL of us. But unless we believe and give ourselves to Him it will do us no good. We have to be crucified WITH Him – take our place in His death by relinquishing our life. And only then are we raised in resurrection union with Him – only then is CHRIST IN US – and only then are we alive in Him.

This is why any gospel that denies, side-steps, or waters down the need for repentance – for the need to come to the Cross and relinquish our life -- is heresy. The fact is, as long as you possess your life you possess death. The only way to HIS life is by repenting of that sin – THE SIN of owning yourself – and passing through death and resurrection in Christ. Then you will be one with Him forever. And because of it, you will be alive in Him forever.

Note those last two words – "in Him." You will find them repeated over and over in the NT – especially in Paul's epistle to the Colossians. God never speaks of eternal life as a THING handed to us independent of union with Christ. No. Rather, again and again, eternal life is said to be IN CHRIST – and we are said to be alive only because we are IN HIM. There is simply no other Truth on this matter.

So what IS eternal life? Well, eternal life is Jesus Christ. Thus, if Christ is in us, we are alive in Him with HIS LIFE. If Christ is not in us, we are dead.

Have we realized that every human being on this planet is, right now, either alive or dead? That every one of us is either dead in Adam, or alive in Christ? There is no in-between condition, for you cannot be halfway born again!

This IS Eternal Life

"Eternal life," is not merely a term that is descriptive of a LENGTH of life. Many of us think of, "eternal life," as a life that never ends. But despite the fact that there is Truth to that thought, it misses the point completely. In the end, eternal life is a KIND of life, rather than a LENGTH of life.

This actually emerges by looking at the Greek words commonly translated, "everlasting," or, "eternal."   Those words do not refer to a length of time.   Rather, they refer to timelessness. Eternal life is a life not governed by time.   It is outside of time because it is the life of Jesus Christ.   It is a KIND of life.

But what KIND of life?   Resurrection life – life that is the result of VICTORY OVER DEATH.   Jesus said, "I AM the resurrection and the life."   Eternal life is the result of being one with the Person who IS the resurrection and life.

Christ in Us

Christianity is CHRIST IN US.   (Col. 1:27)   Oh, how we need to see this Truth! If there is one Truth that has been distorted, misrepresented, and at best, turned into dead doctrine, it is that Truth. Christianity is not a religion, merely a list of doctrines, or just a nice life lived in anticipation of heaven. Christianity is LIFE ITSELF – HIS LIFE IN US. Christianity is CHRIST IN US – and the impact of everything that He means.

Once we realize that Christianity is CHRIST IN US, and begin to understand what this really means, the Bible takes on new meaning. All of a sudden we begin to understand that we really ARE born again new creations – we are now one with God Himself.

Soul and Spirit

But we have this treasure in earthen vessels, that the excellency of the power may be of God, and not of us. (II Cor. 4:7)

Jesus Christ is the TREASURE. We are the earthen vessel. But despite the fact that we are one with Him in spirit, we are not Christ, and Christ is not us. There will always be distinct identities. The Treasure is IN the earthen vessel. What better description could there be of, "Christ IN US?"

As mentioned earlier, when the believer comes to Christ by faith, we are, "joined to the Lord and are made one spirit with Him." (I Cor. 6:17) But we are NOT made one physical body, or one psyche, with Him. These are of our natural man. The physical body is that part of our natural makeup that we can see, and the psyche is that part of our natural makeup that we cannot see. Thus, our spiritual union with Christ creates a separation in us between our spirit that is joined to the Lord, and our natural man that is NOT joined to the Lord. Indeed, the two are contrary one to the other – flesh vs. spirit -- as the Bible states. Each believer has BOTH.

It is a struggle for most believers to know what is OF Christ and what is OF the natural man. But this struggle is resolved in only one way: By coming to know Christ. Then we will know what is NOT of Christ. And since the natural man is the basis of appeal for the enemy, Satan's goal will be to confuse the two – indeed, millions of believers are walking in the flesh thinking that they are walking with Christ. They are deceived.

We need to see that eternal life is not our life. Eternal life is not our natural man given religion. It is not the result of God doing something TO us to bring out our potential. No. That is actually

Gnosticism. In reality, we are NOT BORN into this world with a trace of eternal life. But if we are born again, we have received from the OUTSIDE of ourselves INTO ourselves the Person of Christ. He is the Treasure. We are the earthen vessel.

It is the will of God that our resurrection union with Christ come to govern our natural man. The natural man will not be saved in this age. But through the work of the Cross the power of the natural man will be broken and Christ, our life, will come to govern.

This ought to be good news, because it tells us that WE are not the source of Truth. We need not look to ourselves, to how we function, to how we think, or to whether we succeed, in order to find the Truth. No. In fact, everything about us, at least at first, is contrary to the Truth. But we can look to Christ, as revealed in the Bible, yes, but also as revealed in US. He is the Truth.

Seeing this division is vital because once we begin to discern the dividing of our soul and spirit, we will no longer be tripped up looking at OURSELVES to discover the Truth, but will realize that in Him alone is the light and the life.

Christ is All

When we are saved, we receive ALL of Christ. And in Christ is ALL that God has for humanity. This is why Paul is able to proclaim, "You are complete IN HIM." (Col. 2:10)

Yet we do not yet understand ALL. We do not immediately experience ALL. Rather, the Christian life is a process wherein we come to discover the Christ we have received in fullness. We receive ALL in Christ, but now must grow to know the One we have received.

If you have Christ in you, you have TRUTH in you. Absolutely. For Jesus is not only THE LIFE, but He is likewise THE TRUTH; THE LIGHT. So again – the Christian life is a matter of progressively discovering HIM. To know Jesus is to know the Truth.

We are going to see that these basic Truths of Christ are the foundation of Christianity. They are the revelation of the written Word of God. They are the entire point of the epistle to the Colossians – the entire point of the Bible. Christ in the believer; Christ is our life; in Christ is ALL – this is the Word that God is speaking. God is speaking – God is revealing the Person of His Son, not only TO His people, but IN His people, and ultimately THROUGH His people.

Can we grasp what this means? "Christ in you, the HOPE – the certain expectation – of HIS glory in and through His people." This purpose begins in this age, but is to be fully released in the eternal ages. This is why it is essential to see that Christ is our life; our ALL – and that all that God is doing and will do, is IN Him, BY Him, and THROUGH Him. It means that it is the eternal purpose of God that individuals, and by extension, His church, be expressions and extensions of His Son.

Chapter 9
The Separation of Soul from Spirit

The fact that each believer has two natures within – has the separation of soul vs. spirit – is essential to realize. It merits a bit more of a discussion.

The Soul

Every person to whom the epistles are written is a believer. The epistles are available to all humanity, but they are specifically addressed to those who profess Christ. And since these epistles contain many warnings regarding the lies of the enemy, it proves that the possibility of deception is real – even for believers. Even if we have received some Truth, and have some experience of Jesus Christ, the possibility of deception remains.

Believers are joined to the Lord and are one spirit with Him – Christ is in us. But as we have seen, the old nature remains. The basis for deception in a human being is that old nature – the natural man; the soul or psyche. Our natural man is corrupt. It is not only governed by lies, but it IS a lie. It is not what God originally created.

Despite the continual presence of the psyche nature, it remains the purpose of God that we come into a realization of His Son – that we might come into the fullness of Christ. He wants us to live IN Christ, and then OUT FROM Christ – as our life, and as our Truth. He wants us to ultimately be an expression of Christ unto God's glory. Thus, the goal of the enemy will always be to abort this purpose. He will try to do so using our psyche; our soul. But since the enemy has no authority to simply overpower believers and make them do or believe anything – that leaves the enemy with only one weapon in his arsenal: Deception. The power of the enemy is found in deception.

But how does the enemy deceive believers using our natural man? How does this deception work?

Satan can get us to believe lies because of the lies that are in us. Perhaps not conscious lies, but unconscious lies, based upon ignorance. As we grow up in Adam, we all develop a particular version of ADAM – with our own particular manifestation of the flesh. It is upon our individual flesh that Satan makes his approach.

Satan is always happy when believers commit sin. But most of all, Satan wants to deceive believers into walking with a false Christ under a false gospel. How does Satan deceive professing Christian to do that? By suggesting a Christ whose center of the universe is THEMSELVES. This false Christianity is molded from out of their own flesh; their own nature. It is a Christianity that results in occupation with SELF.

This false Christ can take many forms. But usually it will be a Christ that satisfies and feeds the natural man – that satisfies and feeds RELIGIOUS flesh. Perhaps this false Christ is compatible with self-righteousness. Maybe the false Christ feeds a desire for self-worth.

Perhaps this false Christ will be one who feeds the religious pride, desire for power, and even lust for riches. Or perhaps Satan will offer a Christ that offers us emotional experiences, or maybe an intellectual satisfaction. Satan will get a person to the point where they mistake their natural man for Jesus Christ; for the spirit of God.

Then there is the negative approach of Satan. Satan will create a Christ that makes people afraid. This false Christ will panic people into doing things to keep on his good side. But when everything is said and done, deception always boils down to a lie about the nature and character of God Himself. And then doctrines that agree will emerge.

So, what we see is that in order for a believer to be deceived by the lies of the enemy, there must be a basis for appeal. No one simply believes a lie out of the blue. To embrace a lie there must be a lie IN ME.

Now, no one volunteers to be deceived. When most of us are deceived we are ignorant. Because we do not know Jesus Christ, Satan is able to fill in that blank space with what appeals to our psyche.

No one who knows Jesus Christ needs to remain deceived. Jesus promised that that spirit of God would guide us into all Truth – would guide us into an inward realization of Jesus Himself. That alone is our protection from deception – or our way out of deception that has taken root.

The Flesh

"The flesh," is not merely gross sin. It is really the SELF principle. The flesh is what humanity is outside of Christ. It is essentially self-ownership – and all of the manifestations thereof – the chief manifestation being occupation with SELF.

Each believer continues to carry the old nature – continues to carry, "the flesh." That is why Paul is able to say:

For the flesh lusts against the Spirit, and the Spirit against the flesh: and these are contrary the one to the other: so that ye cannot do the things that ye would. (Gal. 5:17)

Here we see that it is clearly stated that each believer carries BOTH the old and new nature. They are contrary to one another. The old nature is he ground of the enemy, and the ground upon which Satan makes His approach. Christ is the Truth. We need to grow to know Christ and live in Him. That is how we get free from, or avoid o begin with, the lies of the enemy.

To, "walk according to the flesh," means to walk according to ME. It is to live and perceive and choose based on how things affect me; based on my reactions. It is self-occupation – but those deceived don't realize it. To them, their condition is NORMAL.

This preoccupation with self is the only way in which those without Christ CAN live. But it is

exactly the kind of Christianity that Satan wants to create: One that is ME centered – but one which I am deceived into thinking is Christ centered.

There are millions of professing believers who think that how they FEEL is how God feels – or they think that how they FEEL is the Holy Spirit in them. If they are emotional – they assume it is the spirit of God. If they have a thought, or have an imagination – they believe they are being, "led" of God. Everything is defined by SELF. And it is all religious – it is all within their Christian walk. But they are walking according to the flesh.

The fact is, the more we come to know Christ, the more we will be delivered out of preoccupation with ourselves – into a preoccupation with HIM. Why? Because as we grow to know Christ we will see that there is nothing in us – nothing to salvage, nothing worth protecting, and nothing of life. But we will see that Christ is all.

This deliverance from SELF is not a legal system. It is the result of SEEING THE TRUTH – of realizing Christ.

Born From Above

Verily, verily, I say unto thee, Except a man be born again, he cannot see the kingdom of God…Verily, verily, I say unto thee, Except a man be born of water and [of] the Spirit, he cannot enter into the kingdom of God. That which is born of the flesh is flesh; and that

which is born of the Spirit is spirit. (John 3:3-4)

We need to grasp those words, "That which is born of the flesh IS flesh, and that which is born of the spirit IS spirit." Can we see that the two are of completely separate natures?

All who are born in Adam — and that is ALL of humanity — are born OF THE FLESH. But those we can be born all over again from above — by being planted into the death and resurrection of Jesus Christ.

The flesh and the spirit — these are terms that really represent the TWO MEN — Adam and Christ.

Therefore in Adam all die. Even so in Christ shall all be made alive. (I Cor. 15:22)

From this we can see that there really have only ever been TWO, "kinds," of people on the face of this earth -- that have ever lived, or will ever live. There are those who are in Adam, and there are those who are born again OUT of Adam — INTO the person of Jesus Christ. Those are the two kinds of human beings.

How many understand that when you and I are born from above in Jesus Christ, God doesn't bring our Adam life BACK to life? No. Rather, he gives us a NEW life, and it IS a different kind of life -- it's a life with which you and I were not born into this world. It is not OF humanity. Human beings can't produce the kind of life that God Almighty gives us in His Son. We weren't born with it, and we don't have any way of getting it on our own.

Governed by Christ

Therefore, brethren, we are debtors, not to the flesh, to live after the flesh. For if ye live after the flesh, ye shall die: but if ye through the Spirit do mortify the deeds of the body, ye shall live. For as many as are led by the Spirit of God, they are the sons of God. (Rom. 8:12-14)

There are millions of believers who say that God is, "leading them," "speaking to them," or, "revealing to them." Some believers would have you believe that God is talking to them every five minutes, giving them directions as to what they ought to do next. Some even get directions from God for others – or so they say. There are even so-called prophets today who issue daily prophecies about world events, and about the church.

Where do we find ANY of this in the Bible – on any level near what is practiced today? Yes, God can lead people. Yes, God can speak to us. But we have already seen that God is today primarily speaking to His people SONWISE. Yet this is rarely mentioned. God's revelation of Christ in His people has been pushed aside in favor of LEADINGS.

Many point to the above passage from Romans – more specifically to the phrase, "For as many as are led by the Spirit of God, they are the sons of God." But if you look at the word translated,

85

"led," you will find that it means, "governed." And then if you read these words in context, the passage takes on amazing clarity.

Paul in this passage is talking about the dangers of, "walking according to the flesh," over and against the necessity of, "walking according to the spirit." That is the context in which he says, "Those who are GOVERNED by the spirit of God are the sons of God." Can we see that there is a huge difference between getting directions or leadings from God – a big difference between that and a life that is GOVERNED by the spirit of God?

A life that is GOVERNED by the spirit of God is one that is GOVERNED by what the spirit of God was given to do: Bring us into an ongoing inward realization of Jesus Christ. Christ is Whom God is speaking. We are to be governed by God's revelation of Him in us.

What a shallow Christianity it would be to simply get directions or marching orders from God – to simply get messages or prophecies from God – but to NOT KNOW CHRIST. In fact, if we do not know Christ, everything else will be subject to our natural mind – to our religious flesh. And that is why so many folks who claim to have leadings and words from the Lord end up in error. They are not governed by a knowledge of Jesus; not governed by a knowledge of the Truth. They are governed by their own psyche – even if they are sincere. And many ARE sincere – they are sincerely blind to Christ. But the deception is real.

86

God can lead people and speak to people. But primarily He is speaking Christ. We are to be GOVERNED by knowing Christ. How many see that if we are governed by knowing Christ, that we are not going to need, "leadings," "prophecies," and, "visions?" No. For Christ is the Truth.

But millions of professing Christians will not accept that this is how God works. They will not accept that a walk in the spirit is a walk governed by an inward realization of Christ. Thus, they are going to be deceived. Satan will appeal to their psyche – and make it seem as if God speaks to them through that psyche. But God NEVER speaks to us through our psyche. He speaks to us by His spirit through a revelation of Christ.

Here we see the key: To know Jesus Christ. We must come to the cross so that the power of our flesh is exposed and begins to be broken. We must begin to come into an inward realization of Jesus Christ – and to begin to be governed by Him. Then when the enemy makes his approach and tries to appeal to our flesh – we will be able to recognize this and resist.

Chapter 10
The Work of the Cross

The Spirit itself bears witness with our spirit, that we are the children of God: And if children, then heirs; heirs of God, and joint-heirs with Christ; if so be that we suffer with [him], that we may be also glorified together. For I reckon that the sufferings of this present time [are] not worthy [to be compared] with the glory which shall be revealed in us. (Rom. 8:16-18)

The Bible teaches that Christians are going to suffer. Why? Well, believe it or not, suffering for a believer is the result of REDEMPTION. It is the result of the death and resurrection of Jesus Christ being worked out in the experience of God's people.

Note: Suffering does not save us. Rather, suffering that is according to the will of God and an outworking of God's purpose is the result of being saved – of being in Christ.

Those who teach or believe that suffering can never be the will of God for His people are deceived. Not only do they ignore direct scriptural teaching, but they are blind to the purpose of God through suffering. Indeed, Peter wrote that suffering is included in our calling to Christ:

For even hereunto were ye called: because Christ also suffered for us, leaving us an example, that ye should follow his steps. (I Peter 2:21)

So, the necessity of suffering for a Christian is not in question. In fact, Paul tells us that our capacity to experience Christ NOW is dependent upon suffering, and our capacity to reign and rule with Christ is likewise impacted by suffering:

The Spirit itself bears witness with our spirit, that we are the children of God: And if children, then heirs; heirs of God, and joint-heirs with Christ; if so be that we suffer with [him], that we may be also glorified together. For I reckon that the sufferings of this present time [are] not worthy [to be compared] with the glory which shall be revealed in us. (Rom. 8:16-18)

Here we see the word, "IF." Paul says, "IF we suffer with Him that we may be also glorified together." In this, we also see, "Christ in you, the hope of glory." Yet it is all dependent upon suffering WITH Christ.

Now, obviously, God does not require that we simply, "log in our suffering time" – and if we do, well, then He will pay us off with a reward. You hear such nonsense among the unconverted. They say things like, "The greater our suffering is in this life, he greater will be our reward." There is not a shred of Truth to that statement.

Suffering is necessary in the life of the believer – but because IF we yield to Jesus Christ in it, it will result in LESS of us and MORE of Christ. That is Redemption -- or, to put it another way, it is redemption being experienced. Suffering is a work of the Cross. It will crucify the flesh so that there can be a greater release of the life of Christ in and through us.

Note that suffering does NOTHING unless we give ourselves to Christ in it. Even unbelievers suffer. But it is faith and surrender to God that makes the difference.

Losing to Find

If we wish to walk with Christ, and actually experience Him, we are going to have to be crucified with Him. Jesus put this necessity front and center to His disciples:

If any [man] will come after me, let him deny himself, and take up his cross, and follow me. For whosoever will save his life shall lose it: and whosoever will lose his life for my sake shall find it. (Matt. 16:24-25)

There are some teachers that try to make this passage mean, "Put your faith in the Cross." Or, "believe Jesus died for you." But there is simply NO WAY to read this passage with an open heart and come away with such interpretations.

You will note the words, IF anyone would come after Me…" There are no other options if we want to walk with Christ. The ONLY option is, "Deny himself, take up his Cross, and follow Me." Thus, we must put God before self – we must LOSE our lives to Christ – by picking up the Cross that God brings. This is just another way of saying, "Yes,

Christ was crucified FOR you. But now the impact of His death must be experienced – you must be crucified WITH Him. That happens only if you pick up the Cross that God brings into your life."

So, we see that this passage is talking about the Christian walk, and NOT about simply believing that Jesus died for us.

Crucified With Christ

Jesus said that if we LOSE our lives to Him – if we are crucified with Him – we will find Him as our life. There will be a greater release of His life in us. This is the same Truth shared by Paul in Galatians:

I am crucified with Christ: nevertheless I live; yet not I, but Christ lives in me: and the life which I now live in the flesh I live by the faith of the Son of God, who loved me, and gave himself for me. (Gal. 2:20)

Paul obviously knew that Jesus Christ was crucified FOR him. As mentioned, all believers know that doctrine; that fact. But here, Paul says that he is crucified WITH Christ. Indeed, he says that this is absolutely necessary for his proclamation that, "Christ lives in me." So once again we see, "Life from death."

We are born into an Adam race which is contrary to God. We are governed by the flesh – so utterly governed by the flesh that we may not even be aware of it. To us, this is normal. To simply know Christ died for us will do nothing to address that problem and bring us to where Christ is our life in a livable and practical way. The only solution is to be crucified WITH Christ. That happens when we pick up our Cross and follow Christ. In other words, there has to be a DEATH that takes place – not a doctrinal death, and not a death that is never experienced. No. We have to actually experience DEATH to our SELF – not death to our body – and not an eradication of the old nature – but a crucifixion WITH CHRIST that will break the power of death over the person that we are.

Because human beings have a WILL – that means that human beings have a SELF. And when everything is said and done, we must either put SELF before GOD or GOD before SELF. Without being crucified WITH Christ, we will never put God before self. There must come a breaking of SELF under the work of the Cross.

One way to describe, "losing our life to Christ," is to ask God – and we must mean it, and it must be done in faith – we must ask God, "to do whatever it takes to bring us into the fullness of His Son; to do whatever it takes to get His full will in us." That is a prayer God will always answer.

Suffering Unto Freedom

Forasmuch then as Christ hath suffered for us in the flesh, arm yourselves likewise with the same mind: for he that hath suffered in the flesh hath ceased from sin; That he no longer should live the rest of [his] time in the flesh to the lusts of men, but to the will of God. (I Peter 4:1-2)

92

In this passage, Peter declares the same Truth as Jesus – he simply uses other terms. He says that if we, "arm ourselves with the same mind" – meaning the same faith, will, and intent towards God as Jesus – that our suffering will eventually result in freedom from sin.

How can this be? Well, all suffering is intended by God to bring us to where we lose our life – lose our self-ownership -- to Jesus Christ. In the end, that is the goal. But since self-ownership is THE SIN in which all other SINS are rooted, can we see that if we relinquish self-ownership how this is going to set us free, not only from self-ownership, but set us free from all of the other sins that are rooted in it?

Sure. We are wasting our time trying to destroy SINS in our life if we do not relinquish the life in which those sins are rooted. LOSE that life to Christ in suffering and SINS will no longer have the same power. You will find LIFE – and in His life is freedom.

In Christ; With Christ

Another place that shows we must experience Christ in His death and resurrection if Romans 6:

Know ye not, that so many of us as were baptized into Jesus Christ were baptized into his death? Therefore we are buried with him by baptism into death: that like as Christ was raised up from the dead by the glory of the Father, even so we also should walk in newness of life. For if we have been planted together in the likeness of his death, we

shall be also [in the likeness] of [his]
resurrection: Knowing this, that our old
man is crucified with [him], that the body of
sin might be destroyed, that henceforth we
should not serve sin. For he that is dead is
freed from sin. Now if we be dead with
Christ, we believe that we shall also live
with him: (Rom. 6:3-8)

Note these words: "Baptized INTO His death;" "buried WITH Him;" "Planted together (with Him);" "Crucified WITH Him;" "Dead WITH Christ;" "Live WITH Him." Do we think that these are merely LEGAL concepts accomplished by Christ – or do we realize that Paul is saying that because we are in real fellowship with Christ that we are to actually experience Him in His Redemptive work?

Paul also said:

That I may know him, and the power of his
resurrection, and the fellowship of his
sufferings, being made conformable unto his
death. (Phil. 3:10)

Note the word FELLOWSHIP. The same Greek word is often translated COMMUNION. It means, "a having in common." Believers are to, "have in common with Christ HIS death, and HIS resurrection" – all of which is HIS LIFE. In other words, this is to be real and experienced. CHRIST is to be experienced. That is what fellowship means.

Life from Death

But we have this treasure in earthen vessels, that the excellency of the power may be of God, and not of us...Always bearing about in the body the dying of the Lord Jesus, that the life also of Jesus might be made manifest in our body. For we which live are always delivered unto death for Jesus' sake, that the life also of Jesus might be made manifest in our mortal flesh. So then death worketh in us, but life in you. (II Cor. 4:7-12)

Note: ALWAYS bearing about in our body the dying of the Lord Jesus. That is more than simply believing Christ died for us. Rather, Paul is describing the necessary work or impact of being crucified WITH Christ upon the believer – he is showing that only if WE lose ourselves to Christ – only if WE see the death or brokenness of the self life – can we experience Christ; can Christ be seen in and through us.

We saw earlier that the believer is joined to the Lord and made one spirit with Him. We are NOT joined and made one physical body with Him, nor are we made on psyche or soul man with Him. Thus, the work of the Cross through suffering is to break the power and control of the psyche – so that our body and soul might become governed by life of Christ.

You will note that the body and psyche are NOT saved in this age. We are saved only in our spirit because it is only in our spirit that we are joined to Life Himself. But as we come into an inward realization of Christ — and our natural man is broken by the Cross — our body and psyche will come to be governed by Jesus as Lord.

The Necessity of Death Unto Life

Why is death necessary to produce life? Because REDEMPTION requires the death of the OLD nature — so that there can be the resurrection of the NEW. Jesus stated:

Except a man be born of water and [of] the Spirit, he cannot enter into the kingdom of God. That which is born of the flesh IS flesh, and that which is born of the spirit IS spirit. (John 3:5-6)

Flesh, or natural man, or anything that is of the old nature, cannot produce LIFE. It can only produce MORE flesh, which is to say, it can only produce that which is condemned under the Cross. Thus, the flesh cannot fellowship with Christ. The flesh cannot live with Christ in an eternal fellowship. Only if the flesh is crucified can we freely live by the spirit.

Jesus referred to the OT picture of baptism to illustrate this Truth. He was saying, "That which is born of the flesh IS flesh — and nothing that is born of the flesh can enter the kingdom of God. The flesh must therefore DIE — pictured by baptism. Only then can there be a NEW birth — of the spirit of God."

This is REDEMPTION. It is death of the old and a resurrection into the new — IN CHRIST. We must be crucified with Christ and be raised in Him.

The Nature of Things

God is NOT fixing the old creation – He is NOT fixing our old man in Adam. Rather, the old man in Adam died in Jesus Christ at the Cross. The new man was raised in Christ. These are foundational Truths. But they must become ours by experience.

As we forsake ourselves and discover Jesus Christ, we are actually in the process of becoming mature sons and daughters of God. We are being positioned for inheritance. All of this has great value for this age. But the greatest release is for the next age.

And if children, then heirs; heirs of God, and joint-heirs with Christ; if so be that we suffer with [him], that we may be also glorified together. For I reckon that the sufferings of this present time [are] not worthy [to be compared] with the glory which shall be revealed in us. For the earnest expectation of the creature waits for the manifestation of the sons of God. (Rom. 8:17-19)

Chapter 11
The Trial of Faith

That the trial of your faith, being much more precious than of gold that perishes, though it be tried with fire, might be found unto praise and honor and glory at the appearing of Jesus Christ: (I Peter 1:7)

What is a, "trial of faith?" Well, obviously, it is a situation wherein faith is TRIED. But what does that really mean?

What is the purpose of any TRIAL – of any testing? To get to the Truth. So, "a trial of faith," is intended by God to bring out the Truth – to bring out the Truth ABOUT our faith. Is our faith REAL? But just as importantly, is our faith based upon the Truth?

It is possible for a Christian person to know the Truth – at least in doctrine – and to confess that they BELIEVE it. It is possible for a Christian to declare that they trust Jesus Christ. But is that faith REAL?   Or is it merely emotional, or intellectual? It is the TRIAL OF FAITH that will expose the Truth – it will affirm the Truth and will expose the real nature of their faith.

There are also lots of folks who believe religious nonsense.   There are professing Christians everywhere whose faith is firmly planted in LIES. Not only do they believe false doctrines and teaching, but their lives are governed by those falsehoods.   Their faith, from a human standpoint, is real – they DO believe – but their faith is based upon lies. The TRIAL OF FAITH will expose what they believe for the lie that it is, and will likewise expose their faith in a lie for all that it can be: Human faith in falsehood.

These are obviously matters of spiritual life and death. That is why Paul likens faith to, "gold tried by fire." It is valuable as gold before it is tried, but gold that is tried by fire is priceless. It has been proven.

There is, however, a common misunderstanding about this passage from I Peter. Many of us assume that a trial of faith is intended by God to bring out both the good and bad in us – at which point God will separate the bad in us from the good in us – and keep the good. In fact, many believe God will then build upon the good that He finds in us. This is error.

The reality is that a trial of faith is intended by God to separate what is of US – both good and bad – from Jesus Christ in us. What is of US is to be put under the Cross -- and Christ is to be experienced and manifested.

The end result is that there will be pure gold – faith that is solely in Jesus Christ – with no faith in ourselves. Our lives will declare, "Yet not I, but Christ."

Paul had such a trial:

For we would not, brethren, have you ignorant of our trouble which came to us in Asia, that we were pressed out of measure, above strength, insomuch that we despaired

even of life: But we had the sentence of death in ourselves, that we should not trust in ourselves, but in God which raises the dead: Who delivered us from so great a death, and doth deliver: in whom we trust that he will yet deliver. (II Cor. 1:8-10)

Paul was not a novice when he had this experience. But even the most mature of Christians ALWAYS have more to learn. There will always be more of Christ to learn than we can imagine because He is eternal. He is God.

This occasion was a case in point. Whatever this situation was in the outward, we can be sure that the real battle was inward – it is a battle of faith. Paul says so. He says that what came upon them – and the spiritual forces of darkness were certainly involved – he says that it pressed them beyond their ability to deal with it. Now, of course, that is always true of a believer in our humanity. But I would submit that this is not talking about Paul's ability to handle this situation by calling upon his human strength. He would have known the folly of doing so. Rather, this was something that seemed to be beyond Paul's faith. It was so spiritually overwhelming that Paul thought it was certain death.

The trial of faith can be like that. You can find yourself in a spiritual environment wherein it seems as if God has given you over to death. You know you cannot deal with it, and it seems as if God has left you in it. There is no explanation, no understanding, and, it would seem, no options. You are going down under. But then you remember that faith means you must step outside of yourself and the terrible trial and TRUST GOD ANYWAYS.

That is what Paul did. He said the entire situation was so, "that we should not trust in ourselves, but in God which raises the dead." His faith had been proven REAL – but it was faith in CHRIST.

Faith in ourselves is so NORMAL to us. We are so used to it that we easily carry it over into our walk with Christ. We, "trust in our ability to believe." We can, "trust that there is something about us that will obligate God to help us." Or, we can despair because we know we are not worthy of God's help – which is nothing more than a frustrated self-trust. No. In the end, real faith is about putting ourselves aside – both the good and bad about ourselves -- and basing our faith on Christ alone. We believe Him because HE is faithful. God will structure a trial of faith that He intended to bring us into this Truth.

The Way of Escape

Wherefore let him that thinks he stands take heed lest he fall. There hath no temptation taken you but such as is common to man: but God [is] faithful, who will not suffer you to be tempted above that ye are able; but will with the temptation also make a way to escape, that ye may be able to bear [it]. (I Cor. 10:12-13)

We just read Paul's account of his great trial – one in which he thought he was going to die. God did deliver him – Paul did find a way of

101

escape. But what was Paul's way of escape? Did God show Paul how to get out of his trial? No. If we read his account, it becomes clear that the way of escape that Paul discovered was FAITH.

Paul promises that God will not allow you to encounter a trial that is above what you are able to bear. But we just read that Paul encountered EXACTLY that kind of trial – Paul said so. It was beyond his ability. That was the entire point of the trial. And yet Paul told us the solution: FAITH. He was essentially saying, "I could not bear this trial. But by faith I rested the entire thing upon Jesus Christ. He was my escape from having to bear what I could never bear."

Paul is telling us that the, "way of escape," is NOT an escape OUT of the trial. Rather, it is a way of escape WITHIN the trial. Note Paul's words: God will make a way of escape so that you may be able to BEAR IT. Not a way of escape so that we might be able to ESCAPE it – but to BEAR IT. Faith in Christ rests upon Christ; trusts Christ to be our strength. That is a way of escape from any damage the trial can do to us.

The words, "way of escape," in Greek speak of a, "stepping out," or, "exit." But not out of the trial. Rather, out of OUR ability -- into faith in Jesus Christ. This is what Paul said he did, and it is what this passage means.

The Eternal Weight of Glory

For which cause we faint not; but though our outward man perish, yet the inward [man] is renewed day by day. For our light affliction,

which is but for a moment, works for us a far more exceeding [and] eternal weight of glory; While we look not at the things which are seen, but at the things which are not seen: for the things which are seen [are] temporal; but the things which are not seen [are] eternal.
(II Cor. 4:16-18)

There is a contrast in this passage between the temporal and the eternal. And yet, God will use that which is temporal to give us the opportunity to have built into us that which is eternal in Christ.

All of our choices in life – good and bad – are going to pass into history. The results of those choices in this temporal realm are likewise going to pass into history. All that we are in Adam is going to pass into history. All of our suffering for the sake of Christ is going to pass into history. So, let's ask: What will remain? The measure of Christ – the real faith – that has been proven and built THROUGH all that will otherwise pass into history. What will remain is CHRIST IN US.

When all of the trials of faith are finished, what will remain is the faith that was made real. And that what we call, "faith" in the here and now, has an eternal release in the eternal ages that we cannot fully grasp now. It is like a seed that is planted. That which is eternal is in the seed, waiting for full redemption.

The trial of faith is intended by God to make redemption REAL by making faith in Christ REAL. And that which is real is ETERNAL.

Faith Governs All

We look not at the things which are seen, but at the things which are not seen. (II Cor 4:17)

For we walk by faith, not by sight. (II Cor. 5:7)

The same faith by which we are saved is the faith by which we must walk. It is faith, not in my ability to believe, or in my ability to find God, or in anything about myself. It is faith in God – a trust and reliance upon His FAITHFULNESS.

Faith does not mean that I can see God – it means that I know that God sees me. Faith may not know where God is leading, but it is confidence that He knows. To walk in Christ by faith is going to require that we trust Him when everything on the outside of us, and even our own inward temperament, contradicts faith.

In the spiritual sense of the word, I DO come to see Jesus Christ. But this is not a vision, or something I muster up out of my imagination. Rather, it is a spiritual KNOWING – based upon faith. It cannot be documented. If it could be, it would not be spiritual. It is a spiritual relationship between God and humanity through Jesus Christ.

The reason that faith is central to the Christian walk is because God is spirit and we are NOT. He is beyond us. Therefore, during this age, faith is the means by which we are united with God through His Son. The Son of God became a man so that man could be united with God through Him.

Don't misunderstand. Our faith does not unite us with Christ – neither does our faith keep us united with Christ. Our faith believes and embraces the Christ in Whom we are united.

The Bible speaks of the need for Christian to have, "the faith OF Jesus Christ." Herein we find a key. We cannot have the faith OF Jesus Christ for anything except what Jesus Christ has faith for. In short, when we give ourselves to Christ in any situation for HIS will alone, HIS will be there and HIS faith becomes ours – we become one with Him in HIS faith in an active, practical way. This can be applied to any aspect of the Christian life.

Ultimately, the trial of faith is intended by God to bring us to where our oneness with Christ in spirit becomes a positive, active, and practical reality. Faith is NOT a force, but a RELATIONSHIP with God through Jesus Christ – whereby our union with Christ can come to govern all of us.

Chapter 12
Overcoming in Christ

To him that overcomes will I grant to sit with me in my throne, even as I also overcame, and am set down with my Father in his throne.   He that hath an ear, let him hear what the Spirit says unto the churches. (Rev. 3:21)

And they overcame him by the blood of the Lamb, and by the word of their testimony; and they loved not their lives unto the death. (Rev. 12:11)

How does a Christian OVERCOME Satan?

The answer is that we overcome Satan by standing by faith in the One who has already won all victory over Him.   Thus, we are never to engage Satan in a battle to overcome him. Rather, we are to live as those who are already under the Blood, and living out from the resurrection life of Jesus Christ.

To put it plainly: By faith we are to live from a position of victory in Christ. We are not live as those always trying to win victory.

How does God bring us to that place? Not by making us strong. Not by giving us a THING called power – to use in His name. Not by giving us techniques or gimmicks. No. God brings us to the place where we can overcome by reducing us to utter and complete weakness. Only then can

Christ BE our strength. Only then will we live out from Christ in His resurrection life.

Paul had a situation in his life where he lived out this Truth:

> *And lest I should be exalted above measure through the abundance of the revelations, there was given to me a thorn in the flesh, the messenger of Satan to buffet me, lest I should be exalted above measure. For this thing I besought the Lord thrice, that it might depart from me. And he said unto me, My grace is sufficient for thee: for my strength is made perfect in weakness. Most gladly therefore will I rather glory in my infirmities, that the power of Christ may rest upon me. Therefore I take pleasure in infirmities, in reproaches, in necessities, in persecutions, in distresses for Christ's sake: for when I am weak, then am I strong. (II Cor. 12:7-10)*

There is a great principle in what Paul shared out of his own experience. We have NO power given to us because of Christ. Rather, we have been given Christ IN US – and HE is the power of God. (I Cor. 1:24) Therefore, it is only as we are made those through whom His life can flow – by making US weak -- that there can be any power from God.

Can we see that it is only if we are exposed as nothing – through failure if necessary – that we will realize that the victory is ALREADY won in Christ? And that we need only put our faith solely in HIM?

Faith is the Victory

Now, this obviously is a call for FAITH. John declared:

For whatsoever is born of God overcomes the world: and this is the victory that overcomes the world. (I John 5:4)

A common error among Christians is to limit the enemies of God to that which is OUTSIDE of us. But the real enemy is WITHIN US – the old nature and unbelief. It is there that the enemy makes his approach – even if He uses outward circumstances to do so.

What this tells us is that victory is NOT achieved when a situation gets fixed, or even when a sin is overcome. No. Victory is achieved when FAITH is established – which then makes everything else possible within the will of God. The battleground for a Christian is FAITH VS. UNBELIEF. Faith is the victory. Unbelief is defeat.

Faith is the battleground because the victory is already won in Christ. IN CHRIST alone is victory. Thus, we need NOT fight to win. Rather, we need to fight to BELIEVE.

So, we see that the key is not for us to try to muster up faith, or to try to grab the power of God and use it to overcome. Nope. The key is to be reduced to weakness so that we might put our entire faith in Christ alone for HIS will and HIS purpose. If we will do that, then the victory of resurrection life will overcome all the things of death.

Jericho

This great Truth about overcoming – that the believer must operate from a position of finished victory – by faith in Christ -- rather than from a position of trying to win a victory – is aptly illustrated in the OT in the story of Jericho.

The Promised Land was a type and shadow of Jesus Christ and all that God has given in Him – the Promised Land was freely given of God and was to be freely received, possessed, and lived in. It was a finished victory in the eyes of God. But Israel needed to take possession by faith and LIVE IN the finished victory.

Jericho was the first place God told Israel to conquer. As such, Jericho represents the whole of the Promised Land.

A Finished Work

It is important to recall the history leading up to the conquering of Jericho. God had told Israel right from the start that He had given them all of the land – this was never in dispute. It was finished, solely by the grace of God. And Jericho, as the first place Israel encountered, was certainly included:

And the LORD said unto Joshua, "See, I have given into your hand Jericho, and the king thereof, and the mighty men of valor." (Josh. 6:2)

Here we see the type and shadow of God's finished work in Jesus Christ. ALL that God has for humanity is given – solely by grace – in the Person of Jesus Christ. Thus, when we receive Christ at salvation, we have, at that point, received ALL that God has to give. (see Rom. 8:32) But then we must discover and experience – we must come into a realization – of the Christ whom we have already received. This progressive revelation of Christ is the Christian life. The OT type and shadow is this Promised Land that is already given – but must then be experienced and possessed for God.

The land IS given. But the land must be taken and possessed. The land would do Israel no good if they merely acknowledged that God had given it to them -- but had then settled elsewhere. No. They had to actually enter into the land, experience it, and live in it.

You will also note that this was NOT optional if Israel wanted to walk with God. God has specifically called them to live in this land unto HIS GLORY. There was no other purpose.

And here is a vital point to see: The victory of Jesus Christ is not manifested when we get what WE want. It is manifested when God gets what HE wants. And this is eternally GOOD.

God has called us unto salvation in Christ – but unto the greater purpose that we might fully experience Christ and live to His glory. There is no other purpose and no other calling. It is the only purpose into which God will lead.

110

The problem that Israel faced, and that we face, is that there are the enemies of God that are occupying that land. For Israel, it was the heathen tribes who occupied this land in walled cities. For us, it is the old nature – it is natural man. The enemies of God consist of all that is contrary to God – and the flesh is always contrary to the spirit of God in Christ Jesus.

If, when we are saved, the old nature were eradicated, this would not be the case. But the old nature is NOT eradicated – rather, Christ is brought in. We are united with Him in spirit. And the Christian life is a matter of the believer decreasing in that old nature so that Christ might increase. This is another way of describing sanctification or overcoming.

Jesus Christ, by His spirit, is INVADING humanity as a race. This begins when a person receives Christ. But as that person walks with Christ, the Cross must be carried – and the Cross is essential to overcoming the flesh. Only if we are crucified with Christ can He live in us, and we in Him. This is the inheritance. In short, all the God gives in Christ is experienced only as Christ Himself is experienced. Jesus Christ, and all that is in Him, is the inheritance of the saints.

The Initial Refusal to Enter

When God brought Israel through the Red Sea and on to the Promised Land the first time, they refused to enter. The reason was unbelief.

***So we see that they could not enter in
because of unbelief. (Heb. 3:19)***

In this we see a number of principles. First, we see that we cannot take possession of what God has given by grace under any other relationship with Him except faith. We cannot take possession by law, by duty, or by fear. Secondly, we cannot take possession of what God has given in Christ unless we are first living IN, and from OUT OF, Christ – which again demands faith.

So God sent Israel into the wilderness – but not to punitively punish them – but to bring them to the place where they could enter the land by faith. It was in the wilderness that Israel was made – not strong enough to enter – but was exposed as utterly weak. Only then would they enter by faith in God.

Enter In Despite Failures

It is eye-opening to compare the facts between the first time Israel arrived at the Promised Land and refused to enter, and the second time when they DID enter. First of all, the purpose of God had not changed in those forty years. Secondly, the land had not changed – it was exactly the same inheritance. Thirdly, the enemies in the land had not changed. They were the same – just as strong and insurmountable. Fourthly, Israel was just as weak, if not weaker, after forty years in the wilderness as they were forty years prior. So what was the difference? It was FAITH. Despite being exposed weak and unworthy, Israel now believed God.

112

Now, of course, during those forty years in the wilderness, all of that generation of unbelief had died out. Sure. And this is the goal of God when He puts us into a wilderness. His goal is that our natural life; our Adam life, might come under the work of the Cross and that we might take our place in the death of Christ – that we might unconditionally abandon ourselves to Him. Then, you see, it will no longer be about whether WE are strong enough, or good enough, to enter in and take possession of what God has given in Christ. Rather, it will be, "Yet NOT I, but Christ."

So God says, "I know all about your unworthiness for Christ. I have always known you were unworthy – but you did not know it – which is why you continually tried to make yourself worthy. Indeed, I have allowed you to wander in a wilderness to show YOU your unworthiness. But this was all unto the end that you might confess it – and then put your faith on Jesus Christ. There was never any other way to enter into the things of God."

God's Instructions

In Joshua 6, God gives instructions to Israel as to how they are to take possession of Jericho:

And the LORD said unto Joshua, See, I have given into thine hand Jericho, and the king thereof, and the mighty men of valor. And ye shall compass the city, all ye men of war, and go round about the city once. Thus shalt thou do six days. And seven priests shall bear before the ark seven trumpets of rams' horns: and the seventh day ye shall compass

113

*the city seven times, and the priests shall
blow with the trumpets. And it shall come to
pass, that when they make a long blast with
the ram's horn, and when ye hear the sound
of the trumpet, all the people shall shout
with a great shout; and the wall of the city
shall fall down flat, and the people shall
ascend up every man straight before
him. (Josh. 6:2-5)*

What God promised DID happen — the walls of
Jericho DID fall. But if you read these
instructions, there is one point that is absolutely
vital to see: God did NOT command Israel to
ATTACK Jericho. All God required of Israel was
that they BELIEVE that the victory was certain,
and in that faith, compass the city — following the
ARK.

Now, if we consider Jericho to be a type and
shadow of any sin, bondage, or darkness in the
believer — if we realize that Jericho represents
anything that stands between us and the
inheritance in Christ — we will have to come to
terms with a great Truth: This is a picture HOW
God's sets people free in Christ Jesus. We are
never set free from anything by attacking
it. Rather, we are set free by abiding and living
from out of Christ.

Why is this the Truth? Because the victory is
ALREADY FINISHED IN CHRIST. Thus, we need
not, indeed, we must not, try to win that victory
all over again. Rather, we must live in the
VICTOR. And if we do, the walls will eventually
fall.

114

Does this mean we have no choices? Not at all. There will be many choices of faith and obedience. But our choices will not be to try to win the victory. Rather, our choices will be because we know the victory IS won. To put it another way – we will walk as those who are working out the finished victory.

The Ark

God told Israel that the victory over Jericho was certain – it was finished – but not yet experienced. He told them to compass the city by following the ARK. The ARK represents the presence of God in His people – the ARK carried by the priests represents, "Christ in us." Israel was to compass the city following the priests who were carrying the ARK. This represents a walk in the Truth – a walk in Christ. It represents a walk in faith.

God's instructions to Israel carry great New Testament Truth. He told them to encircle the city one time for each of six days. Six is the number of MAN. Those first six days must have seemed so futile! They were walking around in circles and NOTHING was happening. Is this not a picture of humanity coming to the end of itself in an attempt to overcome and purge sin? Sure. That is what God wanted to illustrate. They circled the city in faith for six days – but NOTHING happened.

This ought to be encouraging to us. There are going to be times in the Christian life when we obey God and believe Him and expect victory – but nothing seems to be happening. It will seem

115

like we really are walking in circles. There will be times when we compass, "our Jericho," in real FAITH -- but it all seems to avail nothing. And yet it is not futile. It is all unto LIFE. We are decreasing and He is increasing – in us and through us. We are carrying a Cross around Jericho – just as the priests carried the ARK -- but this death will eventually result in resurrection.

In type and shadow, Israel was picturing what Paul taught in the NT. He wrote to the Corinthians:

Always bearing about in the body the dying of the Lord Jesus, that the life also of Jesus might be made manifest in our body. For we which live are always delivered unto death for Jesus' sake, that the life also of Jesus might be made manifest in our mortal flesh. (II Cor. 4:10-11)

Those six days represent those seasons in which we, "bear about in the body the dying of the Lord Jesus." Nothing is happening – but everything is happening that is essential for victory. "Our Jericho," will only fall if the natural man and flesh is crucified. And once that is sufficiently accomplished – then comes the SEVENTH DAY – the day on which HIS LIFE is made manifest. And His life IS victory.

This is not about getting THINGS from God, or about God changing our situation. Those issues are secondary. Rather, this is about God getting His purpose IN US so that we can take possession of what He has for us in Christ.

When the seventh day arrived, Israel was to compass Jericho seven times. Seven is always the number of God -- the number of spiritual perfection. Six falls short of seven, as does man fall short of God's glory. But that seventh day represented the result of faith in a God who is, "other than," ourselves -- and it brought victory.

Can we see that God needed to see His victory made real IN His people – before those people could move forward in that victory? In other words, Israel had to be reduced to where their faith was solely in God. Then God would work through them for HIS will.

Warfare did not conquer the city. In fact, the only warfare that was necessary was the warfare to BELIEVE. Again, we are never called upon to win a victory. Rather, we are called upon to rest in Christ, who is the victory. Once our faith is mature -- once we arrive at our seventh day -- the battle is over. The walls will come down.

The Aftermath of Victory

Once the walls of Jericho fell, Israel had to go up and take possession of the city – and in doing so – they had to live in that city to God's glory. When we are set free through Christ, that area of our life that had been governed by the flesh must now be governed by Christ. This is where most of our choices of obedience come in -- it is only AFTER the walls fall down and we are free that we are able to obey God. This is Christian living and it is victory experienced.

You will note that Israel destroyed everything in Jericho. This is God's way of illustrating that NOTHING of the old man is carried into the new creation. "Old things are passed over, behold, all things have become new." (II Cor. 5:17) The soul and body will remain as vessels through which Christ can be manifested. But they are not OF the new creation in this age.

Along that same line, Israel was forbidden to take for themselves any accursed thing -- i.e., things that had been dedicated to false gods. And they were forbidden to take for themselves any of the wealth of Jericho. From these instructions we can see that in the aftermath of victory the people of God are to be all the more separated unto God from the ways of this world. The six days, let alone the time in the wilderness, was to make them safe for the seventh day victory.

Overcoming NOW in Christ is a matter of living from the position of victory, and standing pat against all challenges. God wants us to live from out of victory – He wants us to live from out of the position of sitting with Christ in His throne. But the greater realization of this will be in the eternal ages.

Chapter 13
Spiritual Growth

What is spiritual growth? Many believers have been taught that spiritual growth is a matter of God bringing out the best in us – through Christ. Many think that God somehow, "acts upon us," and does stuff to us by His spirit, to make us, "look like Jesus." Others have been taught that spiritual growth is the result of keeping laws and principles that will build various, "character qualities," in us. Still others think that it is nothing more than personality development. All of these are error.

It is amazing how many errors in the Christian church come back to blindness to the reality of CHRIST IN US and blindness to the personal cross. And where there is blindness to these, the enemy will fill in the blanks with a religious substitute that will salvage natural man and reinforce our preoccupation with ourselves.

So what IS spiritual growth? We have already seen the answer. Spiritual growth means LESS of me and MORE of Christ – eventually leading to NONE of me and ALL of Christ. Spiritual growth is the result of being progressively crucified with Christ – resulting in living in resurrection union with Him – such that our lives proclaim, "Yet not I, but Christ!"

This is what Paul was getting at to the Galatians:

I am crucified with Christ: nevertheless I live; yet not I, but Christ lives in me: and the life which I now live in the flesh I live by the faith of the Son of God, who loved me, and gave himself for me. (Gal. 2:20)

Note the words, "Yet NOT I, but Christ." That is spiritual growth. In fact, it is redemption being experienced. And the fact is, it is the ONLY possible outcome of God's plan and purpose. That is not bad news. It is good news -- because it is freedom.

Jesus taught essentially the same Truth to His disciples:

If any [man] will come after me, let him deny himself, and take up his cross, and follow me. For whosoever will save his life shall lose it: and whosoever will lose his life for my sake shall find it. (Matt. 16:24-25)

In order to find, and experience, and live from out of Christ as our life, we must relinquish OUR life. We do so by picking up our Cross. The impact will be LESS of us and MORE of Christ.

A New Creation

Human beings are, by nature, preoccupied with SELF. This is the damage done through the sin of Adam — it is what happened when Adam lost fellowship with God. He was left with only himself — an empty, corrupt, and lifeless shell — subject to the realm of darkness. He tried to fix himself; cover the damage sin had done. But it

120

was to no avail. Human beings have been trying to do the same ever since.

Jesus Christ came – not to FIX the damage done to the human race – not to lift death from the human race – but to satisfy all justice, judgment, and death in Himself. Christ tasted death for all, so that, by faith, we could die in Him – and then be raised in Him a NEW CREATION.

The new creation – resurrection in Christ Jesus -- is not the reversal of a dead person back to the same life. No. Rather, it is the result of passing through death in Christ – and leaving the old life behind IN death -- and then a resurrection unto a NEW LIFE.

What passes through death in Christ? The human spirit. The human spirit is united with Christ and raised in Him – raised in resurrection union. The physical body and psyche are NOT raised in Christ during this age. They remain OUTSIDE of our spiritual union with Christ.

It is the will of God that during this age that we grow to realize, experience, and know Jesus Christ. God wants our minds to be renewed according to Christ – and if it is – then our body and psyche will come to be governed by the Christ who dwells within our spirit. But our body and psyche are never resurrected in this age. They will never be made to, "look like Jesus." Rather, they will be governed by Jesus Christ – they will be vehicles through which Christ is manifested.

There is a reason why this is so important to grasp. Christians by the millions are trying to make their body and psyche, "look like Jesus." We try to do this through works, religious programs, service, and whatever we think will, "build character." But even if we do not realize it, we are trying to effect change upon our outward man. We are trying to feel better, act better – we are trying to mold ourselves according to what we think will, "look like Jesus." We are actually trying to FIX our body and psyche. Yet this is all wrong. It is nothing more than a continuation of preoccupation with SELF – nothing more than another attempt to cover ourselves with, "fig leaves." It is deception.

Can we see where this entire mentality is off the track? We are trying to work from the outside in. But God always works from the inside out. And if we are born from above, JESUS CHRIST is within. Thus, the key to spiritual growth is not to try to make ourselves, "look like Jesus." Rather, it is to put ourselves aside completely – to leave ourselves alone. Instead, we are to ask God to do whatever it takes to bring us into an inward realization of His Son. As we come into an inward realization and knowledge of Christ, we will grow to be more and more occupied with CHRIST. The outward will begin to be governed by knowing Christ.

Paul's Description of Spiritual Growth

We have already seen that Paul's declaration of, "Yet not I, but Christ," is a wonderful description of spiritual growth. But there are others. One of them we touched upon in the last chapter. We need to revisit that passage and apply it to spiritual growth:

> *For we preach not ourselves, but Christ Jesus the Lord; and ourselves your servants for Jesus' sake. For God, who commanded the light to shine out of darkness, hath shined in our hearts, to [give] the light of the knowledge of the glory of God in the face of Jesus Christ. But we have this treasure in earthen vessels, that the excellency of the power may be of God, and not of us. [We are] troubled on every side, yet not distressed; [we are] perplexed, but not in despair; Persecuted, but not forsaken; cast down, but not destroyed; Always bearing about in the body the dying of the Lord Jesus, that the life also of Jesus might be made manifest in our body. For we which live are always delivered unto death for Jesus' sake, that the life also of Jesus might be made manifest in our mortal flesh. So then death worketh in us, but life in you. (II Cor. 4:5-12)*

If you read the above passage, you will see that Christians are never made, "to look like Jesus." There are no programs intended to work upon our outward man.   There are no laws or principles that will build into us the character of Jesus. What Paul is describing is the WORK OF THE CROSS upon our outward man – which will break the power of the outward man – resulting in a person manifesting the Christ Who dwells within.

None of this will make any sense unless we begin where Paul begins in this passage:

For God, who commanded the light to shine out of darkness, hath shined in our hearts, to [give] the light of the knowledge of the glory of God in the face of Jesus Christ. But we have this treasure in earthen vessels, that the excellency of the power may be of God, and not of us.

Paul begins with CHRIST IN US – he begins by pointing to the fact that God wants to continually, "shine in our hearts to give the light of the knowledge of the glory of God in the face of Jesus Christ." That is a mouthful, but Paul is saying that we have the Treasure within the earthen vessel that we are – and that God wants to bring us into a growing realization and knowledge OF HIM. Jesus Christ is the starting point and He is the goal. He is the Alpha and Omega.

Paul then talks about his tremendous trials, which are the work of the Cross. The work of the Cross is intended by God to show us the Truth about ourselves, and if we pick up our cross, to break the power of the natural man. Note that we do not simply pick up our cross every so often – but rather – we carry our cross CONTINUALLY as we follow Christ:

Always bearing about in the body the dying of the Lord Jesus...

Jesus Christ bore our Adam man in His body on the Cross. As we experience being crucified with Him, our physical body and psyche will, "bear about the dying of the Lord Jesus." We will come to know what it means to be, "dead to sin and alive to God."

So, again – we see NOTHING here about working upon our outward man with programs or principles intended to make our outward man, "look like Jesus." We see no suggestion that God will ACT UPON our outward man to create, "Christian character qualities." Rather, we see the outward being brought under the Cross.

Paul then tells us the result of the work of the personal cross:

Always bearing about in the body the dying of the Lord Jesus, that the life also of Jesus might be made manifest in our body.

Is this not exactly what Jesus promised – that if we LOSE our life to Christ that we would FIND Him as our life? Is this not exactly what Paul declared to be the outcome of being crucified with Christ: "Yet not I, but Christ?" Paul is telling us that if we give ourselves to Jesus Christ under the work of the Cross that we are going to experience what it means to be crucified with Him – we are going to, "bear about in the body the dying of the Lord Jesus." But the result will be that, "the life of also of Jesus," will be manifested in and through us.

Can we see that this is NOT a description of how to make our outward man, "look like Jesus?" Rather, it is a description of how God will crucify the outward man so that Jesus Christ Himself – the Christ Who lives IN the believer – might be manifested IN and THROUGH the believer.

But if we are blind to the reality of Christ within, and are blind to what it means to be crucified with Christ, we are going to need to find alternative definitions and explanations for these passages. And those are everywhere today.

Paul concludes this passage with these words:

For we which live are always delivered unto death for Jesus' sake, that the life also of Jesus might be made manifest in our mortal flesh. So then death works in us, but life in you.

"For we which live are always delivered unto death — that the life of Jesus might be made manifest in our mortal flesh." Again — this is the same Truth as found in Galatians 2:20:

I am crucified with Christ: nevertheless I live; yet not I, but Christ lives in me: and the life which I now live in the flesh I live by the faith of the Son of God, who loved me, and gave himself for me. (Gal. 2:20)

All of these passages define for us what spiritual growth really is: Spiritual growth is, "Yet not I, but Christ." Spiritual growth is the death of my outward man under the work of the Cross unto the manifestation of Jesus Christ in and through me.

Chapter 14
Christ, Our Righteousness

The doctrine of, "justification by faith," states that if we put our faith in Christ, God imputes to Christ our sin, and imputes to us HIS righteousness. This is the Truth from a legal standpoint. But in reality, God does not merely impute to us the righteousness of Christ. Rather, God IMPARTS to us Christ Himself. We are joined to Christ and made on spirit with Him. (I Cor. 6:17) When that happens, Christ in us IS our righteousness – the only righteousness that there is for a human being.

It is impossible for a believer to walk in self-righteousness but to rest in Christ as our righteousness at the same time. The former is a lie. It is deception. It is another gospel. It is sin. The latter is the result of experiencing redemption in Christ. It is the ONLY outcome of seeing the Truth and walking with Christ.

Spiritual Circumcision

We have already seen that God must expose our self-righteousness for what it is – He must expose US for what we are. This is the work of the personal Cross. Only then will we voluntarily lose ourselves to Christ – and thus, find Christ as our life. In the OT, circumcision was a type and a shadow of this Truth. It was a type and shadow of the Cross of Jesus Christ – and the fact that we are to be crucified with Him.

Physically speaking, circumcision was a symbolic, "cutting off," of that body part that was used to reproduce the Adam race. In commanding this under the Old Covenant, God was illustrating the New Covenant Truth that through the Cross of Jesus Christ, the Adam race was, "cut off," through death. There would be a NEW creation.

The apostle Paul certainly had to pick up his cross. He had to lose his life. Thankfully, he gives an account of what he experienced in losing his life, and in finding Christ as his life. In that account -- from Philippians 3 -- is a great example for us.

For we are the circumcision, which worship God in the spirit, and rejoice in Christ Jesus, and have no confidence in the flesh. (Phil. 3:2)

No confidence in the flesh -- but rejoicing in Christ Jesus – this is spiritual circumcision. It is the result of seeing the Truth.

Spiritual circumcision includes the cutting off of all self-righteousness. It is a cutting off, through the Cross, of religious flesh – the cutting off of the religious SELF life. But not as a thing unto itself. It is all unto Christ as our righteousness.

With that in mind, we can see why Paul says that, "WE are the circumcision," that is, "we are those whose old nature is under the Cross of Jesus Christ." Then, he gives the result: "We have no confidence in the flesh."

Paul had NO confidence in his flesh, i.e., no confidence in anything about himself before the Lord -- not because God commanded it of him, but because Paul saw the Truth. The Truth is — there is NOTHING in ourselves over which to have confidence before God. If we really want the Truth then that is what we are going to discover. And it will be a condition over which we will rejoice — just as Paul said.

If we will allow God to show us the Truth about ourselves, we will run to the Cross and voluntarily embrace it — because we will be done trying to salvage something about ourselves. We will know that HIS LIFE is the only life that there is.

So, Paul's biographical story as to how he lost his life in Christ begins with this as the framework: There is nothing about us upon which we might stand before God. No. All of that is crucified — spiritually circumcised. But this is cause to rejoice — IN CHRIST JESUS.

Paul's Former Life

Though I might also have confidence in the flesh. If any other man thinks that he hath whereof he might trust in the flesh, I more: Circumcised the eighth day, of the stock of Israel, [of] the tribe of Benjamin, an Hebrew of the Hebrews; as touching the law, a Pharisee; Concerning zeal, persecuting the church; touching the righteousness which is in the law, blameless. But what things were gain to me, those I counted loss for Christ. (Phil. 3:4-7)

129

Paul begins to list all of the religious traits and attributes about himself that pertained to his former life as a Pharisee. There is not one sin listed – these are all the things that he used to think were assets before the Lord. He admits, "These are the things about myself that gave me confidence in the flesh; confidence in myself as being righteous before God."

Paul's admission that he thought that he was BLAMELESS before God – righteous before God because of his law-keeping – stands out among those things he had to lose. What we see in this is that Paul had to lose, not things, but Paul had to lose himself – Paul had to lose, be stripped of, have exposed as a lie, his self-righteousness.

If we are being stripped of our self-righteousness, and are coming to know Christ as our righteousness, we are growing spiritually. We are seeing the Truth.

How does God strip us of our self-righteousness? By exposing it as a lie. In other words, God must allow us to FAIL so we will be faced with the Truth of our complete unrighteousness. But as He does, God will likewise reveal Christ as our righteousness.

The Loss of All to Win Christ

Yea doubtless, and I count all things [but] loss for the excellency of the knowledge of Christ Jesus my Lord: (Phil. 3:8)

Paul says that he suffered the LOSS of his life – of everything about himself – but FOUND the knowledge of Jesus Christ; FOUND Christ as His life and as His only righteousness.

Note the exchange: Lose your life and you will find Christ as your life – but that will always include LIGHT – if Christ is our life then we will KNOW HIM.

People often ask how to come to know Christ. Here we find the answer: Give yourself to Him in an unconditional surrender. Ask God to do whatever it takes for Him to get His will in your life – and then when God does do whatever it takes, live out your surrender. You will come to know Christ.

Romans says:

> *I beseech you therefore, brethren, by the mercies of God, that ye present your bodies a living sacrifice, holy, acceptable unto God,* [which is] *your reasonable service. And be not conformed to this world: but be ye transformed by the renewing of your mind, that ye may prove what* [is] *that good, and acceptable, and perfect, will of God. (Rom. 12:1-2)*

Do you want to know God; know His will. We must get on the altar – carry our Cross daily.

Found in Christ

> *...for whom I have suffered the loss of all things, and do count them [but] dung, that I may win Christ, And be found in him, not having mine own righteousness, which is of*

the law, but that which is through the faith of Christ, the righteousness which is of God by faith: (Phil. 3:8-9)

Paul was FOUND in Christ — but he describes the condition in which he was found in Christ: Not having a righteousness of His own, but that which is through the faith of Christ. Before Paul could BE FOUND in Christ — found with Christ as his only righteousness — he had to lose HIS righteousness.

It ought to make sense to us that the two cannot coexist. We will never find the freedom of Christ as our righteousness, and know Him as our righteousness, if we are still walking in the delusion of our own righteousness.

Do we realize that self-righteousness is a terrible LIE? A mesmerizing deception? Have we seen that it is SIN against God? Another gospel? This matter of righteousness is serious — it is front and center in the Bible, and thus, vital in the life of the believer.

This autobiographic account given to us by Paul was his journey from being a diehard Pharisee to becoming one who could joyfully declare, "Yet not I, but Christ?" At the core was this matter of righteousness. Paul had to lose his righteousness in order to be found with Christ as His righteousness.

Chapter 15
Seeing Jesus Christ through Suffering

The necessity of suffering in the experience of a Christian is so thoroughly established in scripture that it is inexcusable that some false teachers deny it. Today we have those who believe we need only, "speak victory," into our lives and into the lives of others and suffering will vanish. The fact that this never works doesn't seem to make a dent in such deception.

Other Christians falsely believe that suffering is a punishment from God — or that it is the result of having made a mistake along the way. But this is the result of blindness to the purpose of God, and ignorance to the fact that God is a redemptive God. There is always a way back to God by the grace of God in Jesus Christ.

But we have seen that's God's purpose in suffering is to bring us into an experiencing of, and realization of, Jesus Christ. Paul summed it up best:

I am crucified with Christ: nevertheless I live; yet not I, but Christ lives in me: and the life which I now live in the flesh I live by the faith of the Son of God, who loved me, and gave himself for me. (Gal. 2:20)

Paul likewise declared:

Always bearing about in the body the dying of the Lord Jesus, that the life also of Jesus might be made manifest in our body. For we which live are always delivered unto death

for Jesus' sake, that the life also of Jesus
might be made manifest in our mortal flesh.
(II Cor. 4:10-11)

Suffering is supposed to bring us to the place where we LOSE ourselves – abandon our self to Christ. As seen in the passage above from II Cor. 4, the result will be that we will FIND Christ as our life. And as we do, we will discover Christ and increase in our knowing of Him.

The Story of Job

The Bible is filled with direct teaching about trials of faith and suffering in the life of a believer. But sometimes the narratives of the Bible convey the same Truth is a way that is just as profitable. Such is the case with the story of job. In the story of Job, we find revealed God's eternal purpose for suffering in any trial of faith.

There are those who claim that the conclusion that we are supposed to draw from the story of Job is that there is no explanation for suffering. We just have to accept it. But that is not the Truth. Not only have we already seen God's stated purpose in suffering, but the conclusion of the story of Job states plainly why Job was tried. And that purpose is the same as the purpose for which Christians are subjected to trials of faith.

We do not have space to discuss the book of Job in detail. So let's skip to the END of the book of Job and see – ahead of time -- what God's purpose was for Job's great trial. If we can see that purpose ahead of time, then as we hit some pivotal points in the rest of the book we will have some definition, meaning, and purpose.

The Purpose and Greatness of God

Let's ask the question right off the bat: Why did Job have to suffer? And why do WE have to suffer? Well, there is a purpose – and at the end of The Book of Job, in chapter 42 -- that purpose is revealed. The purpose of God in Job's suffering was to bring Him to where he could SEE GOD. The NT correspondence to this is an inward realization of Jesus Christ – leading to finding Christ as our life.. But in order to accomplish this in the life of Job, Job had to be brought to where he was willing to, "lose his life, in order to find it." (see Matthew 16:24)

Towards the end of Job's trial, leading up to chapter 42, God began to show Himself to Job; to reveal HIMSELF to Job. He did NOT end Job's suffering – nor did He reveal to Job, at that point, the answers to his suffering. No. Rather, God revealed HIMSELF to Job. And that is the key. It is the purpose FOR the suffering: That we might SEE Jesus. But in our ignorance, I think most of us want INFORMATION from God as to the WHY we are suffering, or as to what we must do to end the suffering. As was the case with Job, God will be silent to such pleas. He will be silent because He knows that we do not need INFORMATION. Rather, we need REVELATION – we need a REVELATION of Jesus Christ.

And so God was silent to Job for a long time -- but then began to reveal to Job – NOT answers, and NOT information -- but then began to reveal

135

to Job -- HIMSELF. That is a key to the purpose of God, and to suffering.

And Job -- once God spoke to him — says to God in Job 42:1: "I know that You can do everything, and that no thought can be withheld from You." He adds, "Therefore I know that I have uttered those things that I understood not -- things too wonderful for me -- which I knew not."

Job is basically saying, "I said the right words. I taught the right things. But Job is saying, "Yet I didn't really understand WHAT I was saying because I had not, at that point, seen YOU, Lord."

Job confesses that he thought he KNEW God because, "he had all the right facts and teachings ABOUT God." And he DID. But he did not know God Himself. In this there is a lesson for us: It is entirely possible for you and I to memorize the Bible, book and verse -- to know all the doctrines; to write about them -- but to NOT know God.

In Job 42:5 we come to the confession that this entire book of Job builds up to — it is really a summary of the purpose of Job's suffering. And it tells us the purpose of the New Testament Christian's trial and suffering -- what God is after; why He allowing these things to happen to us. Job says, "I have heard of You, God, by the hearing of the ear. I heard ABOUT You, Lord, in teaching and in doctrine." He says, "And all of that was good." He says, "But now my eye sees YOU. Wherefore, because my eye sees YOU, I abhor myself and repent in dust and ashes."

So there it is. What is the purpose of God in suffering for His saints? That we may SEE GOD -- that we may have an INWARD REVELATION OF JESUS CHRIST. That is God's purpose in suffering. The suffering itself is the tool God uses to bring us to the end of ourselves – to break our faith in ourselves – to prove to us by experience that there is no life and no truth in us. Then we can voluntarily turn to Jesus Christ and lose ourselves to Him. We will do so voluntarily because we SEE HIM. And in doing so, we will FIND Christ as our life.

A Good and Upright Man

Now, that is the conclusion. But if we look at some of the build up, we will find some insight into the ways of God with His people. First, Job 1:1:

There was a man in the land of Uz whose name was Job, and that man was perfect...

The word translated, "perfect," means, "mature" or "and upright. God also says, that Job,

"...feared God and hated and avoided evil."

Take note that is not only the inspired Word of God -- so we can believe that this is a description of the true character of Job -- but God Himself is going to repeat this in a few verses. Job was walking in the light that he had – he had been faithful to God. But can we see that this does not mean that Job had ALL light? No. In fact, Job had not yet SEEN GOD HIMSELF. But in the context of where Job was presently in his walk with God, God was able to say this about him.

Now, verse 8:

> *And the Lord said unto Satan, "Have you considered my servant Job -- that there is none like him in the earth -- a perfect and upright man, one that fears God hates evil."*

That's almost a word for word quote of verse 1. God said this and so it is certain that it is the Truth about Job.

Secondly, God Almighty calls Satan's attention to Job. Can we see that? God initiates this.

Thirdly, once Job's trial begins, God says to Satan that Satan, "moved God against Job WITHOUT CAUSE." See Job 2:3.

The point is this: The trial and suffering of Job -- as stated by God Himself -- was NOT because Job had sinned. It was NOT because God was, "punishing," him, even for unconscious sin, such as self-righteousness. There's NO sense here of, "punishment," whatsoever. No. The reason for Job's suffering was to bring Job to the place where he could SEE God. Therefore, his trial was not punishment, but rather, chastisement .

"Chastisement," means to, "train up a child." It is done in LOVE. It's for our betterment. There is no sense here that Job had sinned, and that God was punishing him. This is exactly the case when we are in a trial of faith; when we are suffering. This is stated in Hebrews:

138

And ye have forgotten the exhortation which speaks unto you as unto children, My son, despise not thou the chastening of the Lord, nor faint when thou art rebuked of him: For whom the Lord loves he chastens, and scourges every son whom he receives. If ye endure chastening, God deals with you as with sons; for what son is he whom the father chastens not? But if ye be without chastisement, whereof all are partakers, then are ye bastards, and not sons. Furthermore we have had fathers of our flesh which corrected [us], and we gave [them] reverence: shall we not much rather be in subjection unto the Father of spirits, and live? For they verily for a few days chastened [us] after their own pleasure; but he for [our] profit, that [we] might be partakers of his holiness. (Heb. 12:5-10)

It is possible that we could be walking in the light we have and that God, in His desire to reveal in us His Son, might allow us to be brought into a very difficult trial. Yet the Bible reveals that this is the love of God as a Father – He wants to bring us on in Christ. That was the case with Job, and one of the lessons in the book for us to discover.

Life and Light

God wants us to SEE JESUS – to have an inward realization of Him. But we are all blinded by unbelief. We are blinded by occupation with SELF. We are blinded by our natural minds. Therefore, God must bring into our experience that which will begin to buckle, and eventually

139

collapse, these aspects of our natural man. Of course, we MUST turn to Christ in these matters by abandoning ourselves in an unconditional surrender. That is faith – and the entire point. But if we do, then we will have abandoned OUR life and begun to find HIM as our life.

John wrote:

In Him was life, and that life was the light of men. (John 1:4)

This short verse contains great Truth. From a practical standpoint, it means that if we will lose OUR life to Christ, we will find Him as our life – and this will result in us receiving light. Sure. That is because Jesus Christ is both life and light. It is therefore a fact that the more we find Him as our life, and live out from Him as our life, the more we will see Him and know Him.

Travail Unto Birth

You will notice that the end of the book of Job, that when he got the revelation of God, he was still suffering. It didn't end at that point. Now it eventually did. But from that point Job no longer was going back and forth about it -- because God was his answer. He did not need to ask WHY.

This Truth is contained in something Jesus spoke to His disciples shortly before He was crucified. He spoke a word to His disciples in anticipation of the great trial they would face when He was taken away. He said:

A woman, when she is in travail, has sorrow, because her hour -- or her season of suffering and travail -- *has come.* And so, while she is in the pains of childbirth, that is what her mind is on. He says, *"But as soon as she has delivered the child, she remembers no more the anguish -- because she now sees a man, or a child, is born into the world. (John 16:21-22)*

He is saying here is that when we are in the midst of trials and suffering, it is going to hurt. We are going to suffer. There is going to be anguish and pain. God isn't despising that; He knows it's going to happen. And we don't need to feel guilty about it. In fact, we can believe and trust God – ALL THE WHILE its happening: Blessed are they that mourn, for they shall be comforted."

But all that being said, most of the time we will NOT understand what's going on while we are in the trial. We will not see a reason for it. BUT something is being BORN. Something is being birthed. We are being brought into the fullness of Jesus Christ. There is that birth taking place. Once we begin to see Jesus, then we are going to look back and say, "My God, as much as I was kicking and screaming all the way through this, it was worth it."

The Eternal Purposes of God

There are many other passages that God inspired that go hand-in-hand with what God reveals in the book of Job. Paul wrote:

And if children, then heirs; heirs of God, and joint-heirs with Christ; if so be that we suffer with [him], that we may be also glorified together. For I reckon that the sufferings of this present time [are] not worthy [to be compared] with the glory which shall be revealed in us. (Rom. 8:17-18)

But though our outward man perish, yet the inward [man] is renewed day by day. For our light affliction, which is but for a moment, worketh for us a far more exceeding [and] eternal weight of glory; While we look not at the things which are seen, but at the things which are not seen: for the things which are seen [are] temporal; but the things which are not seen [are] eternal. (II Cor. 4:16-18)

In these passages we see that suffering has an eternal purpose. God uses many vehicles in the lives of His people. But all of those vehicles are going to pass away. What WILL remain is the relationship by faith with Jesus Christ that has been built through those vehicles. And if it is of Christ it is eternal.

The Trial of Faith

Peter wrote:

That the trial of your faith, being much more precious than of gold that perishes, though it be tried with fire, might be found unto praise and honor and glory at the appearing of Jesus Christ. (I Peter 1:7)

142

The trial of faith is exactly that: A trying, really, a PROVING of your faith. This will often mean that God must prove that we are nothing – as He did with Job -- and that HE is everything. Job saw that God was everything when we saw God Himself. When we reach that point we are seeing the TRUTH.

But in the midst of a trial of faith, the faith we have will be contradicted. It will be contradicted by outward circumstances, but it will also be contradicted by the reactions and perspective of our own nature. Yet the entire situation is orchestrated by God so that we might step outside of ourselves – leave ourselves alone – and believe God is faithful despite the apparent contradictions.

This is not a, "test," that God puts upon us to prove to Himself that we have faith. Rather, it is an experience wherein we may see the Truth and be adjusted to Jesus Christ.

In the final analysis, faith is surrender. It is a matter of losing my life for the sake of Jesus that I may find Christ as my life. This is the Truth embedded in the story of Job, and it is God's purpose for a believer. The impacts of it will last from this life into eternity.

Chapter 16
All in Jesus Christ

Redemption is unto SONSHIP. Believers are to become sons and daughters IN the Son.

Note that: IN the Son. There is nothing God has given or will ever do except it be IN and THROUGH Jesus Christ. In other words, Jesus Christ is ALL to the believer.

This primary Truth has immense ramifications. For example, it means that God has not given believers THINGS. He has not given us THINGS that are added to Christ. He has not given us THINGS independent of Christ. No. Rather, God has given us Christ Himself -- **in Whom** are ALL THINGS. Indeed, in Jesus Christ God has given ALL that He has to give.

Does that seem like a strange statement? For the last two thousand years this great Truth has not been widely preached. And yet it is a foundational Truth of Christianity. It is everywhere in the Bible.

For example, Paul writes:

> *Christ, [who is] our life (Col. 3:4)*

That is a very short and simple statement. But it carries tremendous ramifications. To plug it into the above statement: God does not give us a THING called, "eternal life." Rather, God gives us the Person of Christ, Who IS The Life, and who is OUR life.

Eternal life is not a THING, or merely a legal classification that God assigns to us if we receive Christ. Eternal life is a PERSON. Thus, if we receive Christ we receive His life – we become partakers of Him in His life. That is why we are saved.

Another way to say this: At salvation, by faith, we are joined to the Lord and made one spirit with Him. (I Cor. 6:17) But that means we are joined to the One who declared, "I AM the LIFE." We are therefore alive with His life. He IS our life.

The same principle applies to every aspect of the Christian experience. For example, God does not merely give us a THING called, "righteousness," because we put our faith in Christ. No. The doctrine of, "justification by faith," rightly states that if we put our faith in Christ, God imputes to us the righteousness of Christ, because on the Cross God has already imputed to Christ our sin. That is correct in a legal sense. But is Christianity is not merely a legal standing before God. The Truth is, if we put our faith in Christ, yes, God does IMPUTE to us the righteousness of Christ – but more than that – God IMPARTS to us Christ Himself. In other words, we are ONE with Christ in spirit. That makes the Living Christ our righteousness.

Paul states that exact Truth to the Corinthians:

But of him are ye in Christ Jesus, who of God is made unto us wisdom, and righteousness, and sanctification, and redemption: That, according as it is written, He that glories, let him glory in the Lord. (I Cor. 1:30-31)

Can we see that if we have Christ in us — if we are alive with HIS LIFE — that included in His life is ALL?

Sure.   Ask: What is within LIFE?   Well, everything. What is outside of LIFE? Death -- in other words, nothing that is of life.   Thus, if Christ is THE life, then ALL that is of God is in Him.   And nothing that is of God is elsewhere. And the incredible Truth is that CHRIST IS IN US.

If believers are to see the Truth — if believers are to come into an inward realization of Jesus Christ — a fundamental dimension of this will be that we will see and know that Jesus Christ is ALL.   And we will grow to see that He is ALL TO US personally.   There is simply no other outcome of seeing the Truth.

The Essential of Christ as All

In the epistle of Paul to the Colossians there are four warnings to the church — all of which are in chapter 2.   Now, when God gives warnings in scripture, it is because He loves us — it is not because He wants to threaten us or make us afraid of Him. Indeed, these four warnings in the epistle to the Colossians are all for the purpose of keeping us centered in the Person of Jesus Christ.

Being centered in Christ -- and the centrality of Christ as ALL — is not merely a doctrinal matter. Neither is it a matter of making Jesus the central figure in a church service.   Now, all of that is

good and fine and we need to do that --
doctrinally and in a church service. But what Paul
is concerned about in Colossians is that Jesus be
central in our personal lives – that Christ govern
our personal faith. Paul is talking about actually
experiencing Christ. In other words, Jesus Christ
is to BE OUR LIFE. (Col. 3:4)

In Him, By Him, and Through Him

In the first chapter of Colossians, Paul sets the
stage for the warnings in chapter 2 by
emphasizing the centrality of Jesus Christ. Once
he establishes Jesus Christ as the SOURCE of all
for the believer, and the GOAL of God for the
believer -- in chapter 1 -- he then issues the four
warnings in chapter 2 – lest believers would be
led away from Christ as our life into deception.

In chapter 1 of Colossians, starting with verse 14,
you find phrases like, "in Him, by Him, through
Him, for Him," and so forth. It is all about Jesus.
In other words, Jesus Christ is the Alpha and the
Omega. He is ALREADY that – but God wants us
to personally experience Him as OUR Alpha and
Omega, personally. God wants Jesus to be the
Alpha and the Omega of every individual life, of
every church, of every ministry, of every revival -
- if we will let Him.

So, in verse fourteen, speaking of Christ, God
inspires about Him:

***In Whom** we have redemption through His
blood, even the forgiveness of sins. (Col.
1:14)*

Note that small, two word phrase: IN WHOM. This is significant. Why? Because it represents a great Truth that is found all through the New Testament; a Truth that is essential. That great Truth is this: God Almighty has not given us THINGS. He has not even given us THINGS merely, "because of," Christ. What He has done is give us Christ HIMSELF -- in Whom are all things.

What that means, and why that is so important to discern, is that you cannot have things from God – as independent from Christ. You cannot have or experience anything that is of God until you discover and experience Jesus Christ Himself. Why? Because He is the One in Whom those things are, and in Whom all things are given.

That is so vital to see. In fact, the four warnings given in Colossians 2 are given so that believers would not depart from Jesus Christ as ALL – so that believers would not stray from the Truth that only in Christ has God given what He has to give humanity. In short, God has wrapped up all that He has to give humanity in the Person of His Son. In Him alone is given all that God has to give.

We are going to find that in Colossians 2, where these warnings are written, that this Truth is central. If you and I try to get the things of God, or experience the things of God, or experience the spirit of God -- as an aside to Jesus or to make Jesus an aside to that, we are going to be deceived.

Ephesians 1:3 declares the same Truth:

148

Blessed be the God and Father of our Lord Jesus Christ, who has blessed us with all spiritual blessings in the heavenlies, <u>IN Christ</u>. (Eph 1:3)

Paul also says:

Accordingly, He has also chosen us <u>in Him</u>. (Eph. 1:4)

He also says:

<u>In whom</u> we have redemption through His blood. (Eph. 1:7)

Again and again, in Ephesians, chapter 1, we read, "IN Christ," "IN Him," and "IN whom." And that same two word phrase is again and again repeated in Colossians 1 and 2. For example, we read in Colossians 2:

<u>In Him</u> are hid all the treasures of wisdom and knowledge. (Col. 2:3)

It is IN Christ that are hidden all the treasures of wisdom and knowledge. It is only as a person discovers the Person of Jesus Christ that it is possible for them to discover what is hidden IN HIM. Thus, if I try to get wisdom and knowledge without knowing Christ I am going to be deceived. This is the warning of Paul.

Let's continue on in Colossians 1. Paul writes, regarding Christ:

Who is the image of the invisible God, the first born of every creature, for <u>by Him</u> were

all things created that are in heaven, that are in earth, things visible and invisible, whether they be thrones or dominions or principalities or powers, all things were created __BY Him__ and __FOR Him__ and __He is__ before all things. And __he is__ the head of the body, the church: __who is__ the beginning, the firstborn from the dead; that __in all things he__ might have the preeminence. For it pleased the Father that __in him__ should all fullness dwell. (Eph. 1:15-19)

Again, Paul is not merely saying that Jesus Christ has to be at the top of your statement of faith. Rather, as we will read later, because Christ is IN US (Col. 1:27) — because we are joined to the Lord and one spirit with Him (I Cor. 6:17) — because we are united with Christ in resurrection union — because of this great Truth — Jesus Christ is to BE our life. (Col. 3:4) We are to be partakers with Him in His life. Everything that Paul is saying here in this epistle boils down to that. Is Jesus my all? That is the question.

Paul makes an incredible statement in verse 19:

For it pleased the Father that __in Him__ should all fullness dwell. (Col. 1:19)

We read in Colossians 2:9:

(In Christ) dwells all the fullness of deity bodily.

These two verses are exactly the same Truth. Of course, Colossians 2:9, has often been mistranslated. Some translations, including the

150

King James, say, "in Him dwells all the fullness of the GODHEAD bodily." No. That really is misleading. The word translated, "godhead," in the New Testament Greek, ought to read, "DIVINITY." Thus, we are being told that in Christ, the Son of man, the God man, dwelt all of the fullness of God – all the fullness of DIVINITY. In other words, He was fully God and fully man. If that doesn't prove Jesus Christ was God in the flesh, I don't know what could prove it.

The mere fact that in Jesus Christ dwells the fullness of Divinity ought to settle it once for all: We are COMPLETE IN HIM. In other words, if Christ is in us, we lack NOTHING that God has for us. How could we lack anything? HE IS GOD. In Him the fullness of God dwells, and He dwells in US.

This is the Christ that God is speaking – it is the Christ with Whom we are one in spirit. IN HIM God has given all that He will ever give humanity.

Therefore, we need not, and we must not, look to other sources, or other experiences -- or to subsequent experiences -- once we have received Christ. In Christ – by the means of the spirit of God – are the fruits, the gifts, and the means of all ministry. Christ is the Alpha and the Omega.

If we look elsewhere for that which is of God, or try to add to Christ with other experiences, we will be deceived. Paul could not be more clear in His warnings to the church. But has the church heard what God is speaking? Have we heard God's LOGOS?

Chapter 17
Christ in You, the Hope of Glory

In the epistle of Paul to the Colossians, Paul presses home the Truth that IN CHRIST God has given ALL. He presses this Truth home, not to simply establish a fact, but so that believers might put their faith solely in Christ — so that believers might continually draw upon Christ as their LIFE. (Col. 3:4)

Paul's epistles are not merely a presentation of doctrines about Christ. Of course, doctrine is going to emerge. But more importantly, Paul's epistles, as is the rest of the Bible, are a revelation of Christ Himself. It will do us very little good to simply memorize teaching. Rather, by faith we must enter into the reality that those teachings present — we must experience Christ Himself.

As Paul continues in Colossians 1, in verse 24 he speaks about being made a minister of God. We need to look at this in order to see the incredible importance of the Truth being revealed in these chapters. Paul begins by mentioning that part of his ministry is that he suffer for the sake of the body of Christ.

I, Paul am made a minister; who now rejoice in my sufferings for you, and fill up that which is behind of the afflictions of Christ in my flesh for his body's sake, which is the church. (Col. 1:23-24)

He then adds:

> *Whereof I am made a minister according to the dispensation of God — i.e., the purpose of God — which is given to me for you, TO FULFILL THE WORD OF GOD. (Col. 1:25)*

Note those words carefully. Paul was made a minister according to God's purpose. But what was the purpose of God for which Paul was made a minister? To fulfill the word of God. But it wasn't that the existence of Paul's ministry, of itself, was a fulfillment of the word of God. No. Rather, it was the Truth that God revealed through Paul's ministry that fulfilled the Word of God.

We must grasp the immensity of this statement. Paul is saying that the ministry that God gave him was so that through that ministry the Word of God would be fulfilled. The Word of God FULFILLED! The Word of God covers the entire purpose of God for humanity and for creation. In fact, since Jesus Christ IS the Word of God, we might say that God intended the ministry of Paul to reveal and minister all that Jesus Christ had done, and all the Jesus is.

Paul was called for that very purpose. But he was not alone in that calling. In a very real sense of the word, Paul's ministry was a forerunner of the ministry of the entire body of Christ — the ministry of the church as a whole, and the ministry of each individual. The body of Christ is to preach the PERSON of Jesus Christ; to be a manifestation of Christ. But the ministry and the preaching — the fact of it, and the doing of it —

that alone would not fulfill the Word of God. The fulfillment of the Word of God – the fulfillment of the preaching and the ministry -- would happen only as those to whom the ministry touched came into an experiencing of the Person of Jesus Christ.

The fulfillment of the Word of God only begins to be fulfilled when the Word of God is preached. But the real fulfillment happens when what is preached HAPPENS. And what was the Truth that Paul preached – that would fulfill the Word of God? Well, Paul introduces it with the term, "the mystery."

Whereof I am made a minister, according to the dispensation of God which is given to me for you, to fulfill the word of God; [Even] the mystery which hath been hid from ages and from generations, but now is made manifest to his saints...(Col. 1:25-26)

A, "mystery," in biblical terms, means that which WAS hidden, but is NOW revealed. Paul uses that term in other places in his epistles. And so we must ask: What is this great MYSTERY that fulfilled the Word of God, that God wanted preached and brought to pass through not only the ministry of Paul, but also through the ministry of the church?

Christ in you, the hope of glory. (Col. 1:27)

The reality of CHRIST IN US – Christ in believers fulfills the Word of God. Jesus Christ joined to His people in resurrection union – that is the mystery that was hidden from ages and

154

generations past, but was now revealed and made possible through the death and resurrection and ascension of Christ. This great Truth, preached, ministered, and edified, is THE purpose of God for this age.

Now, if we grasp this, and then add to it what we have already seen about Jesus Christ being ALL – that everything that God has to give is given in the Person of His Son – it becomes clear as to the awesome Truth: Because we are joined to the Lord and made one spirit with Him -- this means that we are one with the Person who is ALL. We are partakers of Christ Himself (II Peter 1:4) – and can therefore live from OUT of Him by faith. We can experience Him. We can come into an inward realization or knowing of Him. This is the impact of CHRIST IN US – the great mystery that fulfills the Word of God; that fulfills the purpose of God for this age, extending into the next age.

"Christ in you, the hope of glory," is perhaps the best definition of Christianity in the Bible. All that God does is either unto the realization of Christ within, or unto the building and edification of Christ within. Everything is built upon Christ as the foundation. No wonder the reality of Christ in the believer fulfills the Word of God.

The Fulfillment of the Word of God

Christ in you, the hope of glory: Whom we preach, warning every man, and teaching every man in all wisdom; that we may present every man perfect in Christ Jesus: Whereunto I also labor, striving according to

his working, which works in me mightily. (Col. 1:27-29)

Here we see what ought to be the outcome of realizing and walking with Jesus Christ — the Christ Who is in the believer: Maturity in Christ. The word, "perfect," means, "maturity.

Maturity is Christ means less of me and more of Him — to the point where I am no longer occupied with myself, but occupied by faith in Him. It means that I have come into an inward knowledge or realization of Christ — and have become more and more governed by Him. It means that Christ is my righteousness. He is my all. What used to be doctrines to me out of God's written Word, have become dimensions that I am experiencing out of Christ, the Living Word.

Along that line you will note that Paul preached CHRIST — not merely a message about Christ. Paul preached the Person. And his continual prayer and desire was that all believers would come into an inward realization of the Person of Jesus Christ:

My little children, of whom I travail in birth again until Christ be formed in you. (Gal. 4:19)

The word translated, "formed," means, "to inwardly realize and express." Paul's desire, and we can be sure it was God's desire, was that believers would realize Christ and become governed by that realization.

156

Wherefore I also, after I heard of your faith in the Lord Jesus, and love unto all the saints, Cease not to give thanks for you, making mention of you in my prayers; That the God of our Lord Jesus Christ, the Father of glory, may give unto you the spirit of wisdom and revelation in the knowledge of him: The eyes of your understanding being enlightened; that ye may know what is the hope of his calling, and what the riches of the glory of his inheritance in the saints, And what [is] the exceeding greatness of his power to us-ward who believe, according to the working of his mighty power. (Eph. 1:15-19)

Paul prayed that we would receive the spirit of wisdom and revelation in the knowledge of CHRIST. Read these passages and one has to ask: Is this the desire of our churches today? Is it our desire personally?

All God Has Given is IN CHRIST

Paul continues to express his great desire that believers know Christ in the first verse of Colossians 2:

For I would that ye knew what great conflict I have for you, and [for] them at Laodicea, and [for] as many as have not seen my face in the flesh; That their hearts might be comforted, being knit together in love, and unto all riches of the full assurance of understanding, to the acknowledgement of the mystery of God, and of the Father, and of Christ. (Col. 2:1-3)

157

Paul wants believers to come into, "the full assurance of understanding, to the acknowledgement of the mystery of God, and of the Father, and of Christ." But Paul adds one more phrase which makes it clear that there is only one means and only one source by which believers can come into this understanding:

Christ, _in whom_ are hid all the treasures of wisdom and knowledge. (Col. 2:3)

All of the treasures of wisdom and knowledge are hid in the Person of Christ – the Person of Christ with whom believers are joined in spirit; the Person of Christ who is in us as the fulfillment of the Word of God. All are IN HIM. In short, if you want to know the treasures of wisdom and knowledge, you have to know Christ.

When we are saved, we are joined to the Lord and made one spirit with Him in resurrection union. We are alive because we are joined to Life Himself. In this we see an example of what we stated earlier: God does not give us a THING called, "eternal life." Rather, He give us Christ, Who is THE LIFE, and Who will then become OUR LIFE. (Col. 3:4)

This is the case of all that is given in Christ. When we are saved we are fully joined to Christ – we are complete in Him. There is no more of Christ to receive – we have received all of Him. But we must spend the rest of our lives, and all of eternity discovering the Christ whom we have received. That is why it says that the treasures of wisdom and knowledge are HID in Him – we find what is hidden in Christ to the extent that we grow to realize Christ Himself.

The Desire of God

With this as a background, we can now see why Paul so strongly issues the warnings that he issues in this chapter. He is warning believers, lest they be seduced away from the very purpose of God – resurrection union with the Person of Christ; the realization of Christ as our life; maturity in Christ.

We saw from Galatians 4:19 that it was the prayer of Paul – it was the travail of Paul – that EACH believer come into an inward knowledge and realization of Jesus Christ. Since this is recorded in the inspired Word of God, is this not the heart cry of God Himself? Indeed, is this not exactly what God is speaking? God is not merely speaking ABOUT Christ. God is speaking Christ Himself. He wants to reveal Christ in His people.

But when it pleased God, who separated me from my mother's womb, and called [me] by his grace, To reveal his Son in me. (Gal. 1:15-16)

Yet, where is this preached today? Walk into most churches and this Truth -- that Christianity is CHRIST IN YOU -- is an unknown. Believers are blinded to this Truth – believers are blinded to Christ Himself. The warnings of the apostle Paul have fallen on deaf ears. The One Whom God is speaking is not being heard. May God give us ears to hear! There is no other answer that God has except the One Whom He has given.

159

Chapter 18
The Rock and the Revelation

Before proceeding in Colossians, it seems profitable to back up into the gospel of Matthew. In that gospel there is an event that gives us a foretaste of everything revealed in the epistles regarding CHRIST IN US. The Truth revealed there agrees completely with what Paul is teaching in Colossians.

When Jesus came into the coasts of Caesarea Philippi, he asked his disciples, saying, Whom do men say that I the Son of man am? And they said, Some [say that thou art] John the Baptist: some, Elias; and others, Jeremias, or one of the prophets. (Matt. 16:13-14)

This was a pivotal moment in the life of Jesus — in His dealings with His apostles. But it is significant that Jesus begins with this particular question: "Who do men — who do OTHER people -- say that I am?" The disciples give their answers — they list who other people say Jesus is. There is not a single correct answer.

This question and answer is really intended to set up the next question:

He saith unto them, But whom say YOU that I am? And Simon Peter answered and said, Thou art the Christ, the Son of the living God. (Matt. 16:15-16)

160

There is a point that Jesus is making by asking these two questions. The point is this: It does not matter – as far as your personal relationship with Christ – who OTHERS say that He is. What does matter is who YOU say that He is.

Can we see that Jesus is bringing this question down to a personal knowledge of Jesus Christ? We have already seen that Christianity is CHRIST IN YOU – not Christ in a group, church, or denomination. No. Christ in the individual – and the entire personal experience of Christ that is built upon, and emerges from Christ in the individual. Jesus is opening up the Truth about Christianity in this conversation – He is introducing the plan and purpose of God that will emerge from out of His Redemptive work.

Peter confesses the Truth about Jesus Christ – he said, "You are the Christ (i.e., the Messiah), the Son of the Living God." We can hardly grasp the magnitude of this realization and confession -- because we have heard this story so many times. But this was a turning point in the ministry of Jesus. It was now possible for Him to build upon the Truth they had realized. Indeed, this is exactly what Jesus answered:

And Jesus answered and said unto him, Blessed art thou, Simon Barjona: for flesh and blood hath not revealed [it] unto thee, but my Father which is in heaven. (Matt. 26:17)

With these words, Jesus states a primary Truth of God's dealing with His people. We cannot know Jesus Christ through the efforts of flesh and blood. We cannot muster up the personal revelation of Christ from out of our flesh, natural man, or religiosity. We have nothing within to muster up – we are born into the Adam race with no Truth in us; with no revelation of Christ within. Furthermore, we cannot receive an inward revelation of Jesus Christ from anyone else.

This is why Jesus first asked, "Who do others say that I am?" – and then, "Who do YOU say that I am?" The revelation of Jesus Christ cannot come from others. It cannot come from ourselves. It must come from God Himself. It must come from God -- into us from the outside of us. And yet that is exactly what God wants to give us.

Earlier we saw that God is speaking Christ; God is speaking to us Son-wise. This means that God is REVEALING JESUS CHRIST to believers in an inward way – bringing us into an inward realization of His Son. If we are saved, then Christ is IN US – and the Christian life is a matter of progressively discovering Him. God is speaking that ongoing realization.

This conversation took place BEFORE Jesus died, was raised, and ascended. It took place before Jesus came down via the spirit of God to dwell in these same disciples in Acts 2. But all of the Truth of CHRIST IN US – and God's purpose through Him – is contained in this conversation. Even though they would only later experience the fullness of Christ within, in this conversation we have the Truth of this revealed as a foretaste – and the beginnings of what God would continue to do in Acts 2.

Jesus told Peter that he was BLESSED to see the Truth about Himself. How true it is when a believer begins to see and realize Jesus Christ! But then Jesus adds the following:

> *And I say also unto thee, That thou art Peter, and upon this rock I will build my church; and the gates of hell shall not prevail against it. (Matt. 26:18)*

Again we find another fundamental Truth that is all through the NT. God must first reveal Christ TO us. But then God must begin to reveal Christ IN US. God must speak into us His Son. Everything that God intends to do MUST be built upon the Jesus Christ Who is in us.

We have seen that God has given everything He has to give in His Son. That means that we only discover that which God has given by coming into a realization of Jesus Christ. Or, to put it another way, Jesus Christ is the ROCK upon which everything God wants to do is built.

Note that Jesus said that it was upon HIMSELF – He is the ROCK – that He would build His church. This was His declaration immediately following Peter's confession of Jesus – a confession birthed out of the revelation from the Father. Thus, we see that it is the inward revelation and realization of Jesus Christ – from out of Christ Himself within -- that forms the basis of what God wants to build.

Jesus said that it was upon HIMSELF – His life and the revelation of Himself to us – that He would build His church. The word for, "church," is EKKLESIA. It means, "called out ONES."

The church is not a building or denomination or congregation. The church are the called out ONES – in other words, called out individuals. Again we see the personal, individual, one-on-one emphasis. We are NOT in Christ because we are in a church. We are NOT in Christ through anyone else. Rather, we are in the church because we are IN CHRIST.

Jesus is declaring that He will BUILD INDIVIDUALS upon Himself – upon the ongoing personal revelation of Himself. And because Truth in Christ is eternal, the gates of hell – all of the power and authority of the enemy – cannot stand.

Just as the writer of Hebrews declared that God is speaking to us through an ongoing, inward revelation of Christ, so Jesus had declared this Truth years earlier. Just as Paul declared that Christianity is CHRIST IN US, so did Jesus begin to reveal this reality years earlier. And just as Paul declared that it is God's desire to reveal Christ in us, so did Jesus declare that it was upon Himself that He would build all things of God.

These are primary Truths that cannot be denied. And they are declared and defended throughout the written Word.

Chapter 19
When Pentecost Came

And I will pray the Father, and he shall give you another Comforter, that he may abide with you forever; [Even] the Spirit of truth; whom the world cannot receive, because it sees him not, neither knows him: but ye know him; for he dwells with you, and shall be in you. I will not leave you comfortless: I will come to you. Yet a little while, and the world sees me no more; but ye see me: because I live, ye shall live also. At that day ye shall know that I [am] in my Father, and ye in me, and I in you. (John 14:16-20)

But ye shall receive power, after that the Holy Ghost is come upon you: and ye shall be witnesses unto me both in Jerusalem, and in all Judaea, and in Samaria, and unto the uttermost part of the earth. (Acts 1:8)

What happened when Pentecost had, "fully come," in Acts 2? There is widespread teaching in the church to the effect that the disciples were already saved at that point – and that what happened in Acts 2 was a SECOND experience which has come to be called, "the baptism with the Holy Spirit." This teaching forms much of the basis for the Pentecostal/Charismatic movement. But it is also accepted in other denominations and churches as well.

This is NOT what happened in Acts 2. But let's discover what DID happen by getting back to a few basics:

165

Salvation under the New Covenant happens when a person is joined to the Lord – when Christ comes to dwell in a person. HE is Life and unless we are made one with Him in spirit we are not alive with His life. Therefore, before Acts 2 no one had Christ within them – no one had been saved under the New Covenant. This proves that Acts 2 was NOT a second experience in addition to salvation. Rather, it WAS salvation received – because those disciples received CHRIST WITHIN through the means of the Holy Spirit.

Jesus Himself stated that the spirit of God had been WITH them, but not IN them – but would be IN them, pointing to the promise that was fulfilled in Acts 2. So before Acts 2 Christ was not IN them, and the spirit of God was not IN them. It is therefore conclusive that they were not saved.

Jesus also continually stated that the spirit of God could NOT be given to them until AFTER He ascended. This affirms that they did not receive the spirit of God until Acts 2.

What about John 20:22?

And when he had said this, he breathed on [them], and said unto them, "Receive ye the Holy Ghost." (John 20:22)

This is easily explained. Jesus breathed ON them, but not IN them. He was affirming that God was WITH them. Only in Acts 2 would there be an INDWELLING.

166

Now, we have to face something here: Jesus said that the spirit of God COULD NOT, and WOULD NOT, be given until AFTER He ascended. At this point in John 20, He had NOT ascended. In fact, that very day He told Mary that He had NOT yet ascended. So if we want to demand that Jesus gave the Holy Spirit to the disciples in John 20 BEFORE He ascended, we are making Jesus contradict Himself.

The answer is as stated. In John 20, Jesus merely breathed ON them – affirming to them that God was with them – which they needed to hear during what, for them, was a very traumatic and uncertain time. There would be no indwelling by the spirit of God until Acts 2. This makes Acts 2 the FIRST TIME in history that Jesus Christ ever came to dwell in humanity through the means of the spirit of God.

Before Acts 2, the disciples were saved under the Old Covenant – their faith had been in the Messiah who was yet to come. They eventually saw that Jesus was that Messiah. After Jesus died, was raised, and ascended, faith in Christ made it possible to become one with Christ in spirit. This is what happened in Acts 2.

Acts 2 was not only the first time anyone received Christ within through the spirit of God, but that means it was also the first time anyone was born from above. It was likewise the beginning of the church – which consists of those who are IN CHRIST. In addition, it was the beginning of the New Covenant.

The Old and New Covenants

Note the promise of God of the New Covenant:

Behold, the days come, saith the Lord, when I will make a new covenant with the house of Israel and with the house of Judah: Not according to the covenant that I made with their fathers in the day when I took them by the hand to lead them out of the land of Egypt; because they continued not in my covenant, and I regarded them not, saith the Lord. For this [is] the covenant that I will make with the house of Israel after those days, saith the Lord; I will put my laws into their mind, and write them in their hearts: and I will be to them a God, and they shall be to me a people: And they shall not teach every man his neighbor, and every man his brother, saying, Know the Lord: for all shall know me, from the least to the greatest. For I will be merciful to their unrighteousness, and their sins and their iniquities will I remember no more. In that he saith, A new [covenant], he hath made the first old. Now that which decayeth and waxeth old [is] ready to vanish away. (Heb. 8:8-13)

Central to the New Covenant was that the New Covenant was an INDWELLING. You can see that in the above description of the New Covenant given in prophetic language. This agrees completely with what Jesus said, that the spirit of God had been WITH them, but would be IN them. The New Covenant began in Acts 2 when Christ came to dwell in them through the spirit of God.

168

The Old Covenant was a type and a shadow of Jesus Christ. The New Covenant was Christ Himself in His people. Acts 2 brought to this to pass – brought to pass the great mystery that Paul preached – the mystery that had NOT been revealed to ages and generations past, but now was revealed – the mystery of CHRIST IN YOU, the hope of glory. (Col. 1:27)

John the Baptist

John the Baptist was not only the last prophet of the Old Testament, but in a very real sense, he and his baptism represented the Old Covenant. John said that he was the voice crying in the wilderness to make way for the Lord. That is exactly what the Old Covenant was.

We certainly see the transition from the Old Covenant to the New Covenant in the baptism of John giving way to the baptism of Jesus. John said:

I indeed baptize you with water unto repentance: but he that cometh after me is mightier than I, whose shoes I am not worthy to bear: he shall baptize you with the Holy Ghost, and [with] fire. (Matt. 3:11)

Can we see the contrast in these words? John's baptism was being replaced by the baptism of Jesus. Instead of being symbolically baptized in water, people would now be baptized into Jesus Christ with the spirit of God. There were NOT to be two baptisms – one into Christ and another with the Holy Spirit. But there is ONE baptism (see Eph. 4:5) into Jesus Christ by the means of the spirit of God.

Baptized Into Christ

Know ye not, that so many of us as were baptized into Jesus Christ were baptized into his death? Therefore we are buried with him by baptism into death: that like as Christ was raised up from the dead by the glory of the Father, even so we also should walk in newness of life. For if we have been planted together in the likeness of his death, we shall be also [in the likeness] of [his] resurrection. (Rom. 6:3-5)

Being baptized into Christ is how we come to be IN CHRIST. It is how we are joined to the Lord and made one spirit with Him — we are baptized by one spirit into one body. This ALL happens at salvation. There is NO second experience.

If we receive Christ within at salvation, but must go on to a second experience, this means that Christ within is NOT enough; Christ is not ALL for the believer. It means that if we have Christ within — but have not received a second experience — it means that we are lacking. In short, Christ is lacking.

The New Testament teaches that the baptism with the Holy Spirit IS the baptism of the believer into Jesus Christ. In fact, all through the New Testament, the indwelling of Christ and the indwelling of the spirit of God are used interchangeably:

170

But ye are not in the flesh, but <u>in the Spirit</u>, if so be that the <u>Spirit of God</u> dwell in you. Now if any man have not the <u>Spirit of Christ</u>, he is none of his. And if <u>Christ [be] in you</u>, the body [is] dead because of sin; but the <u>Spirit [is] life</u> because of righteousness. But if the <u>Spirit of him</u> that raised up Jesus from the dead dwell in you, he that raised up Christ from the dead shall also quicken your mortal bodies by <u>his Spirit that dwells in you.</u> (Rom. 8:9-11)

There are seven references to Jesus Christ within by the means of the spirit of God in these verses. There are NOT two indwellings – but ONE – Jesus Christ in us through the spirit of God.

When Pentecost fully came in Acts 2, the Person of Jesus fully came by the spirit of God to dwell in His people. This was the promise of the Father. It was the fulfillment of the Word of God – the great mystery finally revealed of, "Christ in you, the hope of glory."

Chapter 20
The Danger of Spiritual Seduction

The Truth that Paul has presented in the beginning of his epistle to the Colossians – the same Truth we have seen in Matthew 16 -- form a basis for the rest of the epistle. Paul has pressed home the great Truth that CHRIST IN US is the reality that has fulfilled the Word of God. It is the purpose towards which God had always been working in generations past, and since Acts 2, Christ within His people is the foundation upon which all that God has been building.

But alongside of the reality of CHRIST IN YOU, Paul has established the result: CHRIST IS ALL. Jesus Christ dwells in each believer, but in Christ is ALL that God has given to humanity. That is gather up in one statement: Christ, our life. (Col. 3:4)

The remainder of Colossians 2 contains a series of warnings as to the dangers, and the deceptions of the enemy – ALL of them intended to blind believers to Christ by presenting, "another Christianity. These are intended to deceive Christians into a walk that is not IN CHRIST – not of HIS LIFE – but is along the lines of dead religion, or the mind of the world. Indeed, it really does not matter in what deception Christians are found as much as it matters that they are not found in fellowship with Christ.

None of us will get far in the Christian life unless we come into the reality of Christ within – unless we begin to live in CHRIST, and out from CHRIST, as our life. It is therefore, a certainty that the

172

enemy will make this reality his primary target. And is this not what we have seen over the last two thousand years? CHRIST IN YOU is virtually an unknown. The foundation of Christianity has been made almost anything else.

The enemy cannot destroy the victory of Jesus Christ. But Satan does retain the power to DECEIVE. Therefore, the enemy will seek to REDEFINE the meaning of Christianity. He will seek to BLIND Christian people to the reality of CHRIST IN US – by presenting alternatives and substitutes.

We see examples of this in scripture – most notably in Galatians, Corinthians, Jude, and Revelation. And in Colossians, Paul issues four warnings against that which would come against the great Truth that he has established: CHRIST IN YOU, the hope of glory.

In Christ is ALL

The series of warnings we find in Colossians 2 are given over and against some aspect of Truth in Christ that Paul declares. The pattern we find is that Paul will say, "Here is the Truth in Christ – but beware – because here how the enemy may seek to redefine or corrupt it."

So, in looking at the first of the series of warnings given by Paul, we must first note the Truth Paul has established – so that we can better understand the efforts of the enemy is seeking to hide that Truth. Paul states this great Truth:

IN HIM are hid all the treasures of wisdom and knowledge. (Col. 2:3)

But notice the warning:

And this I say lest any man should beguile you with enticing words. (Col. 2:4)

If Paul is saying that IN Christ are hid all the treasures of wisdom and knowledge, then what would Paul be warning us against? He would be warning us against, "enticing words," that would suggest to us that the treasures of wisdom and knowledge are found elsewhere -- other than IN Christ.

We MUST grasp what Paul is revealing in this passage. IN CHRIST is ALL that God has to give. But there will be enticements to find what you need elsewhere. Now, note that when these enticements are presented, they are not presented as a source for what you need INSTEAD of Christ. No. They are presented AS Christ – or AS the will of God. And people will take the bait if they are blind to Jesus Christ and the Truth that is in Him.

We have to note something here -- that there are all kinds of treasures of wisdom and knowledge out in the world. There is math knowledge and knowledge of science. There is nothing wrong with either. But these are not the treasures of wisdom and knowledge that Paul is to here referring. In context, he is talking about spiritual wisdom and knowledge. In Christ alone are all the treasures of spiritual wisdom and spiritual knowledge. In other words, it is the knowledge

174

of God, the knowledge of reality, the knowledge of Truth.

Paul is writing this lest any man should beguile us with enticing words. "To beguile," means to, "deceive by false reasoning." It is to deceive into a wrong thinking. In addition, the word, "enticing," means to lure with bait. So Paul is warning against false teachers who would lure us with bait into false thinking and reasoning. Of course, this is more than just a one-time occurrence. It is a matter of being lured into a completely false position; a false mindset that begins to interpret God, the Bible, and Christianity.

One example of this would be so-called modern prophets. There are people who post daily prophecy on the internet – they claim to be hearing from God on a daily basis about just about everything under the sun.

Ask: If IN Jesus Christ are hid ALL the treasures of wisdom and knowledge – if that is REALLY true -- then would God appoint prophets to whom He speaks for the rest of His people? No. God is speaking CHRIST IN ALL. We read earlier that God USED to speak through prophets but NOW is speaking in HIS SON – IN WHOM are hid all the treasures of wisdom and knowledge. Do we believe that or don't we?

But you see, if Christian people do NOT believe that then they will not only be open to hearing from God through these so-called prophets, but will even seek them out. They will indeed be BEGUILED – and won't even realize what is

175

happening to them. They won't realizing that such nonsense is keeping them from a personal relationship and experience with Christ for themselves.

Is Christ IN YOU personally, or is He not? Is Christ the only Mediator for us all, or not? Do we have personal and individual access to God through Christ, or not? Or do we need special people to hear from God FOR US?

These are not theological questions. They are questions of spiritual faith, life, and Truth.

Someone is liable to say, "Well, this prophet said things and they came to pass!" So what? Listen to the words of God in Deuteronomy:

> *If there arise among you a prophet, or a dreamer of dreams, and gives thee a sign or a wonder, <u>And the sign or the wonder come to pass, whereof he spake unto thee</u>, saying, Let us go after other gods, which thou hast not known, and let us serve them; Thou shalt not hearken unto the words of that prophet, or that dreamer of dreams: for the LORD your God proves you, to know whether ye love the LORD your God with all your heart and with all your soul. (Deut. 13:1-3)*

Obviously, a prophet is proven false if what they say does NOT come to pass. But here we see that a false prophet may speak a word that DOES come to pass. But in that case, what makes that prophet a false prophet? What makes them as false prophet is that they use even their accuracy to lead you into a false position – they lead you into a false Christianity – they blind you to the fact that God wants you to know Christ for yourself, and to know Him as your source of wisdom and knowledge. THAT is the issue – and it is the warning of Deuteronomy 13.

Note the mention of signs and wonders in this warning. The mere suggestion of a sign or wonder from God will draw in Christians like a magnet. Few test the spirits. Few doubt whether what is going on is of God. We see this with most of the false revivals that have occurred over the last few decades. Experiences have taken the place of the Person of Christ.

Another good example of this might be the Word of Faith heresy. False teachers lure in victims by offering them financial blessing – and many take the bait because of either need or greed. And many begin to become, "programmed," by these false teachings to the point where it distorts their knowledge of God. The bait worked because of either ignorance or unbelief in themselves – but that is precisely why we have to come to know Jesus Christ

Another example is to replace faith in Christ with intellectual knowledge or philosophy. People get degrees in Biblical theology but never come to know HIM.

Some of us are susceptible to things like philosophy, the occult, spiritualism. I don't think most of us would deliberately jump into those things in an open handed rebellion against God. But I think that we can get to the place where we do seek for spiritual knowledge – out of desperation – and we might even seek God in those things.

Now, don't think that such practices are so out of the question today -- because it is happening right now in segments of the Body of Christ. Some people are practicing breath prayers, contemplative prayers, sitting around almost like they are in a trace. I've seen it. Professing Christians sitting around with their hands open, almost like people do in yoga, and they are breathing deeply and chanting over and over the same phrases. Those phrases are prayers and they think that if they concentrate really hard that they will contact God. It is almost like they are trying to summon God to come down.

Then there are heretical movements like, "The Shepherding Movement," and ministries like Bill Gothard – both of these teach the same destructive doctrine of, "submission to authority." They teach that unless you are, "under authority," you are exposed to the realm of Satan. They teach that you have no direct personal relationship with Jesus Christ, but must go through your authority.

All of these things, and there could be listed dozens more, are the result of being blinded to Jesus Christ by enticing words that are carried by spiritual deception. And when folks are blind to Christ then Satan is easily able to bring in a substitute that looks like God's will.

The solution is exactly what Paul has stated: ALL is given in Christ. And we are free to experience Christ directly, individually, and personally.

178

Indeed, Paul stated many of the same things on this matter elsewhere in his epistles:

He that spared not his own Son, but delivered him up for us all, how shall he not with him also freely give us all things? (Rom. 8:32)

Now we have received, not the spirit of the world, but the spirit which is of God; that we might know the things that are freely given to us of God. (I Cor. 2:12)

So, that is the first warning of Paul in this epistle: That God has freely given us all that He has to give, including all of the treasures of wisdom and knowledge, in His Son — but only in His Son. Thus, discover and come into a realization of Jesus Christ and you will unfold all that God has put in Him. Try to discover the Truth, or try to discover God Himself, through any other means and you will be deceived.

Chapter 21
By Grace Thru Faith

The second warning by Paul is actually embedded within this statement of Truth:

As you have therefore received Christ Jesus the Lord, so walk in Him. (Col. 2:6)

The warning is clear: Do not try to walk with Christ in any way that is different from, or contrary to, the means by which you received Him. Thus, we have a very simple question: How do believers receive Christ? "By grace through faith." (see Eph. 2:8-10) Sure. We received Christ solely by faith in Him. So, Paul is saying, "Therefore walk in Christ by the same Truth: By grace through faith."

Is this Truth followed? The vast majority of churches and ministries loudly proclaim that we are saved by grace through faith. But then once people embark upon the Christian life many of those same churches and ministries teach that they have to be under the law. How widespread that is in the Christian church!

Tithing is a good example of that. "Oh, we are saved by grace -- but you need to tithe or God is going to curse you." Or some will teach, "We are saved by grace but it won't mean anything unless you get delivered from a generational curse that is over your life that you did not know anything about." All of these are lies. No, we receive Christ solely by grace through faith and that is

how we need to walk with Him.   There is NO
other Truth and no other way to walk in Christ.

Another Gospel

It would seem that most believers do not take
these matters seriously.   And yet read the words
of the apostle Paul:

> *I marvel that ye are so soon removed from
> him that called you into the grace of Christ
> unto another gospel: Which is not another;
> but there be some that trouble you, and
> would pervert the gospel of Christ. But
> though we, or an angel from heaven, preach
> any other gospel unto you than that which
> we have preached unto you, let him be
> accursed. As we said before, so say I now
> again, If any [man] preach any other gospel
> unto you than that ye have received, let him
> be accursed. (Gal. 1:6-9)*

This passage ought to get our attention.   But
nevertheless, you have large pockets of the
Christian church walking in some form of law;
dead religion; or outright legalism.   Paul does not
mince words.   Being under the law is ANOTHER
GOSPEL.   To walk in ANY form of law is equal to
standing aloof from Christ – which is the Greek
meaning behind the words, "removed from Him
that called you."   Later, he would tell the
Galatians that they had, "fallen from grace."   He
would say, "Christ is of no effect for you." (see
Gal. 5:4) In short, if we walk under the law –
which would be to walk contrary to the Truth of,
"by grace through faith" – we will NOT be walking
in Christ.   As it pertains to our actual Christian

181

life, we will be standing outside of Christ as our life.

We tend to limit being, "under the law," to being, "under the penalty of the law." But that is not what the Bible means by the term. To be, "under the law," means that my faith is in something about MYSELF, rather than solely in Christ. I am trying to maintain my righteousness or standing before God on the basis of something about ME. It could be good works, or my supposed character, or some act of faith that I have performed. But if my relationship with God is NOT based solely upon Jesus Christ then it already is upon MYSELF. That is the default.

We need to understand that a life of faith is not one that merely accepts the historical facts that Jesus died, rose, and ascended FOR us. Certainly faith DOES believe and accept those as the Truth. But the life of faith is in the LIVING CHRIST who accomplished those historical acts. We are IN CHRIST. Christ is OUR LIFE. Thus, we are to live in and out from the One who carries all of these redemptive realities in His very Person. That is what it means to WALK in the same Truth and grace by which we are saved.

There is not one aspect of Christ that saves us and another by which we walk. No. We were saved and walk with the same, unchangeable Person. Therefore, to proclaim that we are saved, "by grace through faith," and then to fashion a Christian life according to law is error. It really is ANOTHER gospel. In other words, it is NOT the Truth.

182

Obeying the Truth

O foolish Galatians, who hath bewitched you, that ye should not obey the Truth, before whose eyes Jesus Christ hath been evidently set forth, crucified among you? This only would I learn of you, Received ye the Spirit by the works of the law, or by the hearing of faith? Are ye so foolish? having begun in the Spirit, are ye now made perfect by the flesh? (Gal. 3:1-3)

Here we see exactly the same deception pinpointed by Paul to the Galatians that we are seeing he pinpointed to the Colossians. The Galatians were SAVED by grace through faith. They began in their walk with Christ on the basis of faith. But now the Galatians were seeking to grow spiritually by keeping laws. That is deception. It is unbelief. It is another gospel.

As noted, the issue here is more than whether we believe in the historical acts of Redemption. Indeed, the issue is more than whether we believe we were saved, "by grace through faith." Rather, the issue is the Christian life – the issue is our relationship with Christ. The Galatians knew all of the doctrines of salvation by grace through faith. But they were seeking to maintain their righteousness before God, and seeking to grow spiritually, by the means of works – by the means of something about themselves.

One example of this today is what is commonly referred to as, "character development." Many teach that we are to grow, "to look like Jesus."

They provide various do's and don'ts — in other words, various laws and principles — that, if followed, will accomplish this and build into us that which will make us look like Christ. Some even turn, "character development," into a checklist that will determine our reward in heaven. But the entire thing is deception. It is all based upon something about US. Life in Christ is redefined into oblivion.

Despite the fact that true Christian growth is a matter of LESS of me and MORE of Christ, believers by the millions still walk as if Christian growth is MORE of US — and they believe if we keep laws that God will actually achieve more of US. They don't use those words, of course, but that is the bottom line.

This is the error against which Paul is warning the Colossians. He is saying, "You were saved by grace through faith. That is the Truth upon which all that God does in Christ is based. Never depart from it. You were saved by grace through faith — therefore live in Christ by grace through faith."

To the Galatians, he is saying, "You were saved by grace and not by works. But now you are trying to become mature in Christ by works and not by grace. That is another gospel. You have fallen from grace and are standing aloof from Christ Himself as your life."

You will note that Paul is warning the Galatians to OBEY THE TRUTH. How many of us realize that, yes, Christians are to obey God — but that behind all of our outward works there must be an inward relationship with Christ that is based upon the

TRUTH? To put it another way, all good works in the Christian life are supposed to be the outcome of living in Christ, "by grace through faith." If my works are NOT — then as noted, the default is that I am doing works in unbelief and not faith.

God has freely given us all things in Christ solely by His grace. Thus, if our obedience is to the Truth, then it ought to likewise be by grace. We ought to obey with no strings attached — with no bargains to offer, nothing to earn, nothing to gain. Freely we have received of God, thus, now freely give of ourselves — that ought to be the motivation behind obedience. Indeed, it is the only motivation behind obedience that makes obedience to be according to the Truth.

A Christian obeys God, not to do for ourselves what Jesus has already done for us — and not try to be IN OURSELVES Who Jesus already is in us — but a Christian obeys God because Christ is our life. HE is our ALL. We cannot add or subtract from Christ. We must simply believe and receive.

Freely Given

Freely ye have received, freely give. (Matt. 10:8)

Jesus gave this instruction as He was about to send out His disciples to minister for the first time in His name. But it a really a summary as to how we are to live the Christian life.

John the Baptist declared:

"A man can receive nothing, except it be given him from heaven." *(John 3:26)*

And as we saw earlier, Paul stated:

He that spared not his own Son, but delivered him up for us all, how shall he not with him also freely give us all things?
(Rom. 8:32)

We can earn NOTHING from God. And it is UNBELIEF to try. But until God reduces us down to where we see ourselves, and the Truth on this matter, we are going to try. We are going to present to God something about ourselves that we think merits His grace. Much of what God is doing in this age in His saints is to get us to where we will FREELY receive what He has FREELY given.

But if we have FREELY received by grace all that God has FREELY given in Christ — then there has been a work of the Cross in us to make that possible. It is really a work of grace. Then we will be able to FREELY give back to God, and out to others, all that God has FREELY given to us. There is actually NO other outcome possible if we have been set free into the Truth on this matter. It is all of grace — FREELY given and received.

Herein we see what Paul was so adamant about this matter. This is not about walking in the right belief system as opposed to the wrong one. No. It is about walking in the Person of Jesus Christ. Grace is His character. Thus, if we want to experience and walk with Him, it is all of GRACE.

186

Chapter 22
Rooted and Built in Christ

To the Colossians, Paul next declares this Truth:

Rooted and built up in him, and established in the faith, as ye have been taught, abounding therein with thanksgiving. (Col. 2:7)

This is a wonderful picture. It be, "rooted," in Christ means that He is our life source. He is our ALL. And to be, "built up in Him," means that we grow spiritual from out of the fact that we are rooted in Him as the source. So, once again we see that Christ is ALL.

Now, with that as a background, here is the next warning:

Beware lest any man spoil you through philosophy and vain deceit, after the tradition of men, after the rudiments of the world, and not after Christ.

Paul is listing some things that will UPROOT us from Christ as our life; from Christ as our ALL. He is warning us that these things will NOT build up IN CHRIST — but will suspend, if not destroy, what God wants to build in the believer.

That word, "spoil," means, "to be carried off as spoil." But notice: Paul is not simply warning about the world seeking to carry us off away from Christ. In context, he is talking about the spirit of the world invading the church. This is a danger from WITHIN. This warning is about a false Christianity – one that carries the name of Christ, but is a dead, religious system passed off as Christianity. It consists of philosophy, vain deceit, and of the basic principles of the world.

Paul says that such a religious system is, "not after Christ," that is, is not OF Christ; FROM OUT OF Christ. Christ is NOT the source. They are not the result of HIS LIFE, and not the result of living in Him. They are completely outside of Christ.

Notice the tie in to the previous warning by Paul that we must walk in Christ under the same grace by which we were saved: We were not saved by a philosophical argument. No one can be brought to repentance through logic. No one can use the methods of the world, staple the name of Christ on them, and set people free. Rather, these methods that Paul mentions are contrary to the grace by which we are saved. They do not root us in Christ, nor build us up into Christ.

Yet look at what so many churches practice today. Many use psychology. Some have 10-step programs they say will lead to freedom from sin. Others form accountability groups. More and more churches practice transcendental meditation, breath-prayers, and chanting. Some actually have a labyrinth woven into a carpet and have people walk it, saying it will have a wonderful spiritual impact upon them. Some television ministries offer anointed oil, cloths over which they have prayed, and various trinkets that they say is, "a contact point for faith." Some of these things are of the occult. Others are simply rituals that belong to dead religion. Still others are simply the ways of the world being brought into the church. NONE of them are of CHRIST. They are not of resurrection life. They are not of the spirit of God.

How many churches today operate almost exactly like a worldly corporation? Almost all of them do. They operate like the world in financial matters. They hire pastors as employees – requiring education over spiritual life. They buy property and hand it to God and expect Him to pay for it. They go on campaigns, advertise, raise money – all in the name of Jesus – thinking He will help them – but none of it is according to Christ. He is in very little of it.

So many believers think that, "trusting God," amounts to the philosophy of, "God helps those who help themselves." We work and serve in the name of Jesus and assume that God will automatically help us because we are doing it in His name.

There are believers who ask, "Well, what is wrong with these things. Don't they help people?" The fact that this question is even asked to begin with identifies the real problem: We do not know Christ. We are not walking, "by grace through faith." We are not ROOTED and BUILT in Him. And where that kind of ignorance is present, the substitutes of the enemy easily find a place.

IN CHRIST – in the Person of Christ -- is hid all the treasures of wisdom and knowledge. But no one can obtain that wisdom and knowledge through philosophy, or thinking, or reasoning. Rather, a person has to come to Christ by faith and take their place in His Cross and be joined to Him in resurrection union. The wisdom and knowledge is then progressively revealed as Christ is revealed.

In other words, Christ is the SOURCE. He is the personification of all Truth and all Light. HE is made to be unto us, WISDOM. (I Cor. 1:30) Thus, we MUST be ROOTED IN HIM as our personal source.

The Vine and the Branches

What better picture of being, "rooted in Christ," and, "built up in Christ" -- which speaks of GROWTH – what better picture could we find other than the picture Jesus gave of the Vine and the branches?

I am the vine, you are the branches: He that abides in me, and I in him, the same brings forth much fruit: for without me you can do nothing. (John 15:5)

In John 15, Jesus is not discussing being saved vs. being lost. Rather, the entire passage is addressed to the saved. Jesus is talking to those who are already branches, and talking about their relationship with Him as such.

He says, "I AM the Vine, and YOU are the branches." That is the relationship between Christ and those in whom He dwells. Note that: It is THE relationship. It is the ONLY relationship there is. Any other attempt at relationship with Christ is not according to the Truth.

190

Jesus is actually giving a picture of CHRIST IN US – or if you prefer, a picture of the believer IN CHRIST. He is our LIFE. He is our SOURCE. He is our ALL. Just as the Vine is to the branches.

That is why Paul declares that we must be, "rooted in and built up," in Christ. This is the only way to live and walk in the Truth – as a believer who is IN CHRIST.

Ask: What is the nature of this relationship? Dependence. But not merely dependence upon Christ for THINGS. Rather, dependence upon Him for LIFE. And dependence upon Christ for Truth.

Can we see that in this picture of the Vine and the branches that we are not given merely a THING called life, but we are given Christ Himself – Who IS our life? We see Christ AS the life of the branch. The Vine is the life – and consequently the source of all pertaining to life – for the branch. The Vine is the ONLY source of ALL.

Jesus told us, "Lose your life to find true life in Me." Can we see how this directly relates to this picture of the Vine and the branches? We cannot hold to our life and expect God to equip our life with things, blessings, and purpose – when it is only the true life IN CHRIST that carries these potentials. No. We have to lose possession of ourselves. We have to come to the Cross and take our place in His death. And then we have to be risen with Christ as our only life. In HIM ALONE are all things that God has for man.

Many sincere Christian people have assumed that God is going to bless THEIR life. He is not. He has already told us to LOSE our lives. The blessings of God are found on in the Vine – only in HIS life. This is not maybe. It is the only Truth.

The Vine is the life source for the branches – that is, the branches partake of, and live from out of the Vine. Again – Christ doesn't merely give us a THING called life – no – Christ gives us Himself. He IS our life. This necessitates the severing of OUR life. But it is the only relationship and reality we are going to find if we go on in the Truth.

The Branches

The picture that Jesus gives of the Vine and the branches carries much Truth that is intended to impart to us an understanding of the real relationship we are to have with Him. The first thing we note is that the branches share he life of the Vine – or – the Vine IS the life of the branches. The branches do not contribute life to the Vine. The branches do not have a separate life of their own.

Imagine the nonsense of trying to bring life to a branch with some means other than the simple fact that the branch is abiding in the Vine. There are NOT other means. Yet, in the body of Christ, we try to bring life into the members with that which is of natural man and the world. The simple answer is that we are IN CHRIST – we are rooted in Him and can only be built up from that union. We must abide by faith IN HIM.

Now, that is simple. We have all heard it. But do we truly recognize what it really means to abide in Christ by faith? It means that we completely by pass our own worthiness — whether we think ourselves good OR bad — and to the completely disregard of ourselves, we take possession of Christ as our Vine. We base this on nothing about ourselves, but simply upon His offer or promise. Nothing more. It is because all is of grace that we can abide in Him.

Now, someone might ask: Well, ok, but how do we know that this will work? How do we know that Jesus will actually be our life? The answer? We know because He is faithful who promised. Do we think there is any other reason? And why would we need another reason? He promised. He is faithful. And so regardless of whether we understand HOW, we can be sure that in Christ is all life and Truth,

Jesus also said, "Without Me you can do nothing." Do we believe Him? I believe if you read the passage you will see that He also means, "Without Me you can be BE NOTHING." And He also means, "You will accomplish nothing but using something other than Me." Sure. What is a branch without the Vine? Dead. You will wither spiritually.

God has never based the life of Christ upon us. He does not need us to, "jump start Jesus." He does not need our input. He simply tells us to believe and abide.

In this day and age of the Word of Faith heresy, believers have been taught, "to believe God FOR what they want." They have been taught to speak or declare victory over things, people, and into their own lives. But God has never promised to honor such nonsense. He is faithful to us according to His own purpose and will – and we ought to be eternally grateful that He is.

We are to be rooted in Christ – in other words, we must realize that we are IN HIM. HE is our life. But if we do, then we will know that HE is our source of all that God is building of Himself in us. Philosophy, natural thinking, psychology, and human wisdom is not the source. They are not of Christ.

Can we see that being BUILT UP in Christ is aptly illustrated by the fruit of the Vine? The branches bear the fruit of the Vine. But the fruit is not of the life of the branch – it is of the life of the Vine – the life in the branch IS the life of the Vine. Thus, all of the fruit of the spirit in the believers life is Christ manifested. It is HIS LIFE manifested through a branch.

Many believers are deceived because they do not know the difference between the fruit of the spirit and natural fruit. Many think that personality enhancement is spiritual fruit. We think that Christians that have outgoing personalities must surely be filled with the joy of the Lord – when in fact it may only be a natural personality trait. There are even unbelievers who are calm and peaceful; who everyone likes and who like everyone. None of it is of Jesus Christ.

This lack of discernment is why many believers are trying to produce fruit through religious methods. Some go to seminary thinking that a degree with build in them spiritual fruit. Some take, "discipleship classes." Some go to Christian psychiatrists. Some attend personality development classes. Others attend 10, 12, 15 step programs to freedom. Others ask for prayer that some, "generational curse," be lifted. Others think that to participate in a worship service is going to produce in them spiritual fruit. But Jesus said NO. The only way in which we can bear fruit is to abide IN HIM by faith. And then what is produced will not be an enhancement of our natural man. What will be produced is a crucifying of our natural man, giving way to the manifestation of Jesus Christ through the Vine.

So there we have another warning. We are to be rooted and built up in Christ — by the same means by which we were saved. We were saved, "by grace through faith." We are to be rooted and built up by abiding in Him by faith.

Chapter 23
Freedom From Sin

There is a difference between being forgiven FOR sin and being delivered FROM sin. Forgiveness FOR sin means I am no longer under condemnation for sin. Deliverance FROM sin means that I am no longer sinning. Thus, when we speak of freedom from sin we are talking about deliverance from sin.

Freedom of sin is achieved by first BELIEVING. The doing – the obedience -- will emerge. But unless our faith is in the One who is the personification of all victory – we will never find freedom.

Yet what does it mean to put our faith in Christ as our Deliverer from sin? Is this just a doctrine? If so, there will be no freedom. To actually be set free from sin I must have a living faith in the Living Christ.

The Place to Start

Deliverance from sin is NOT POSSIBLE unless a person puts themselves and their conduct aside – bypasses themselves completely – and puts their FAITH solely in Christ. Only then will we be delivered, and only then will our attitude and conduct eventually line up with Christ.

And yet so many of us get this backwards. We focus first on how we behave. And then, if we think our works are satisfactory, we feel free to believe. And when that is the case we are doomed to defeat.

So much of our reason for wanting to be delivered from our sin is our preoccupation with ourselves – with our continual quest for self-righteousness. Thus, faith in Christ becomes secondary. Instead, our faith is in ourselves. We would never admit that, but that is why it is deception And it is why, when we are under such a delusion, that God must let us fail. He must bring us to the end of these things that will never result in freedom.

God must bring us to the place where we see that we have NO HOPE for freedom other than through Jesus Christ. We have to be brought to that place because it is only then that we will be able to put real faith that is SOLEY in Christ.

So it must be repeated: We have to put ourselves and our sin aside and put our faith solely in Jesus Christ despite ourselves. We have to put our faith in Christ for freedom BEFORE we are free. When else would we put our faith in Christ? Do we that we must free ourselves from sin before we can come to Christ? Then why would we need to come to Him at all?

The Real Battle

If you ask the average Christian, "What is the real battle in the Christian life?," many will say, "Our struggle with sin." So many of us live in the vicious cycle of trying to obey God, and yet failing -- then feeling condemned -- and then trying harder -- only to fail again. The battle never seems to end.

The problem here is that we think the battle is to fight sin and win the battle. We think that this is what God wants us to do – and that we have power in Christ to do it. But it does not work. Why?

It does not work because we are fighting the WRONG BATTLE. The primary battle for believers is not with sin. The battle is FOR faith.

Christian cry out and develop methods to be delivered from sins. But what we really need is deliverance from unbelief.

Unbelief is not usually a refusal to believe Christ. Often, it is trust in someone or something OTHER than Christ – including ourselves, or perhaps our religious practices. But anything that keeps us from believing Christ is unbelief.

Again, the answer is faith that is solely in the Person of Jesus Christ. We MUST put our own righteousness aside and believe Christ despite our failures. That is so simple. It is the ONLY path to freedom. And it is clearly revealed in scripture – it is what God HAS spoken.

Mortify Sin

For if ye live after the flesh, ye shall die: but if ye through the Spirit do mortify the deeds of the body, ye shall live. (Romans 8:13)

Mortify therefore your members which are upon the earth; fornication, uncleanness, inordinate affection, evil concupiscence, and covetousness, which is idolatry. (Col. 3:5)

198

The word translated, "mortify," in this verse means, "to destroy by neglect." Paul is here affirming the key to freedom from sinning: We do not get free from sin by fighting sin. Rather, we leave sin alone because we believe Christ. If we believe Christ and abide in Him we will discover what God already declares: We are DEAD to sin but ALIVE to God.

> *Knowing that Christ being raised from the dead dies no more; death hath no more dominion over him. For in that he died, he died unto sin once: but in that he lives, he lives unto God. Likewise reckon ye also yourselves to be dead indeed unto sin, but alive unto God through Jesus Christ our Lord. (Rom. 6:9-11)*

Paul is simply telling us to believe and walk in the Truth of Redemption in Christ. We will always commit sins -- but the Truth in Christ never changes. Therefore, EVEN when we sin Jesus Christ remains our righteousness – and therefore EVEN when we sin we can keep our faith in HIM.

If we are truly DEAD TO SIN, and ALIVE TO GOD, then why would we need to engage sin in a battle? Why would we need to win an already finished victory? Why, if we are dead to sin and alive to God, would we live as if we are alive to sin and dead to God? No. Leave sin alone – EVEN when you sin -- because you believe.

Now, the possible misunderstanding here is that we can, "sin because grace abounds." Someone could think that to, "leave sin alone," means that we need not obey God. No. The issue here is what we are to do about our sinning. Paul is telling us that we need to BELIEVE the Truth – and that if we believe the Truth we will discover by experience that IN CHRIST we are free from sin. The outcome will be obedience that is OUT FROM faith.

Many believers try to, "obey God," not because they believe, but because they don't. They are trying to make the Truth to be true by their conduct. Paul is telling us that we don't need to make the Truth to be true by our conduct – we need to believe the Truth regardless of our conduct. If we do, then we will discover by experience that the Truth is true.

To the extent that we bypass our own conduct and righteousness and ABIDE BY FAITH in Christ, we will experience freedom from sin. That is because we will be living in HIS LIFE.

One example – perhaps a bit mechanical – is to consider abiding in Christ to be, "plugged into Christ." If by faith we are plugged into Christ His life flows into us and through us. Sin will have no place. But if we focus upon trying to defeat sin we will be in unbelief and won't be plugged into Christ. We will actually be plugged into, and under, the law. And all of the consequences of being under the law will flow into us. We won't be plugged into Christ.

Losing to Find

Then said Jesus unto his disciples, If any [man] will come after me, let him deny

200

himself, and take up his cross, and follow
me. For whosoever will save his life shall
lose it: and whosoever will lose his life for
my sake shall find it. (Matt. 16:24-25)

What does it mean to LOSE your life to Christ? It means to abandon yourself into His hands – for whatever it takes for Him to get His glory. We do this as to overall commitment, but then it must be worked out when we pick up our Cross daily. Our Cross is whatever will result in us losing our life to Jesus Christ. God initiates our Cross. We cannot.

But although we don't usually think of it as part of losing your life to Christ – we must lose our self-righteousness. Self-righteousness is a HUGE part of the natural life – the life we must lose. At the core of self-righteousness is self-ownership – self-rightness is self-ownership. It is unbelief. For a professing Christian it is a matter of trying to do for ourselves what Christ has already finished.

Freedom from sin is certainly the field in which self-righteousness is most often lived. Christians try and try to obey themselves free from sin. They bring in religious gimmicks and practices. None of them accomplish anything except to reinforce the sin.

It is a waste of time to try to get free from SINS unless we abandon to the Cross the ground in which all sins are rooted: Self-ownership and unbelief. Lose THAT and sins will begin to fall away.

Lose your life to Christ — this will include losing our self-righteousness. This is a big part of what it means to DENY ONESELF. That includes LOSING any delusion that we can do a thing about ourselves and our sin. What we must do is the one thing Jesus tells us to do: Lose our lives to Him. Reckon ourselves dead to sin but alive to God — in other words, believe and rest in Christ.

Faith in Christ

Believers everywhere are praying for deliverance from sin. But even if we have good motives in doing this, it is based in error. We do not need deliverance from sin. Rather, we need deliverance from unbelief. In Christ there is already freedom from sin. Believe that. Pray to see that. Get free from unbelief and the sins that entangle us will lose their grip.

I say again — we must FIRST abide in Christ by faith despite our sins in order to find freedom from sin. But if we try to FIRST fight sin in order to abide in Christ we are in error — we are under the law; we are in unbelief. We will simply empower sin all the more through our unbelief.

So what is the real warfare? Faith vs. Unbelief. No struggle with sin is ever won unless that battle of faith is won. Faith is our victory — a faith that emerges out of the realization that there is nothing I can do to fix myself — but the realization that in Christ it is finished.

Chapter 24
Complete in Christ

After Paul warns the church to beware of those who would carry us off out of Christ as our life, he then makes another declaration – in which is embedded yet another warning. He writes:

> *For in him dwells all the fullness of the Godhead (Diety) bodily. And ye are complete in him. (Col. 2:9-10)*

Can we see that within this declaration of Truth that Paul is warning us against any teaching to the effect that we are NOT complete in Christ? Absolutely. For every Truth there is a contrary error. Jesus Christ is the TRUTH. The enemy is the father of lies.

Note that IN CHRIST is all the fullness of DIETY. The word, "Godhead," is not correct, and not once appears in scripture. It should always be translated either, "Godhood," or, "Deity." In other words, the fullness of God Himself -- of all that God the Father is -- dwells IN Christ – dwells in the God-man. We cannot find a more direct statement in the Bible to the effect that Jesus Christ is God.

But there is more. Paul has already told us that Christ is IN US. So, if the fullness of God dwells in Christ, then, "You are complete in Him." Or, to put it another way, if Christ is ONE with the Father, and we are ONE with Christ, then we are ONE with the Father through Him.

203

We cannot take the declaration, "You are complete in Him," lightly. It carries immense ramifications. It goes back to a Truth stated earlier. If we are in Christ – joined to Him in spirit in resurrection union – then we have in Christ all that God has to give. God has given us ALL things freely in Christ. Thus, there can be NOTHING that God has to give that we lack.

Also as noted earlier, despite the fact that we have ALL of Christ and ALL that is IN Christ – we receive ALL of Him at salvation – the Christian life is a matter of discovering and experiencing the Christ that we have fully received. For example, we have to discover the treasures of wisdom and knowledge by growing to KNOW HIM. But that being the case, if we have received Christ, we have received all that God has to give.

Now, in saying that we are complete in Christ, Paul is echoing what he is declaring in this chapter – the Christ alone is to be our source for all. Did we receive ALL of Christ at salvation, or only a part of Christ? We received ALL of Christ – and so AS we have received Him – walk in Him. Walk, knowing that, yes, you have much to discover – but you do not have to try to receive more from God. You must simply discover the Christ you have received.

All is in Christ

Paul is warning us about the dangers of seeking more of the things of God from other sources than Christ, or by means other than that of faith in Christ. This error is everywhere. A primary example of this error is when believers seek a

SECOND experience in addition to receiving Christ that has been called, "the baptism with the Holy Spirit." Many believe that it is only in this second experience that we receive power to live the Christian life, to serve, along with all of the gifts. In other words, we must ADD to Jesus Christ with what we receive in this second blessing – meaning we lack those things if we have ONLY received Christ.

Let's ask: Is it possible to become one in spirit with the Living Christ – with the One who said, "I AM the Alpha and the Omega, the first and the last, and the beginning and the end," but nevertheless LACK what God has to give? Is it possible for Christ to be our LIFE – and EVERYTHING is in HIM -- and still lack what speaks of the spirit of life? Is Jesus Christ NOT enough – such that unless we go on to receive this baptism we will be lacking?

What in the world do we think Paul meant when he wrote, "We are complete in Him?" Did he mean that we lack -- unless we add to Christ? That the One who said, "I AM the Alpha and the Omega," isn't enough?

He that spared not his own Son, but delivered him up for us all, how shall he not with him also freely give us all things? (Rom. 8:32)

All Things Given in Christ

In saying that God has given us all things IN Christ, we are really saying that Jesus Christ IS all of the things of God IN the believer. Of course, for He is the LIFE.   He is the TRUTH. Everything else is within those realities.

One declaration of Paul that shows that Christ is all the things of God in the believer is found in I Corinthians:

That no flesh should glory in his presence. But of him are ye in Christ Jesus, who of God is made unto us wisdom, and righteousness, and sanctification, and redemption: That, according as it is written, He that glories, let him glory in the Lord. (I Cor. 1:29-31)

You will note: God does not give us wisdom. No. He gives us Christ who IS unto us wisdom.   In other words, wisdom is the outcome of knowing Jesus Christ and having your mind renewed according to the Truth.   Likewise, God does not give us a righteousness of our own to possess within ourselves. Neither does He merely impute to us a legal righteousness.   Rather, God IMPARTS to us Christ Himself – we are joined to Jesus Christ and HE is then our righteousness. Sanctification is not the result of God acting upon us doing things to us to make us holy.   No. Sanctification is the result of our natural man, and our self-ownership being crucified so that Christ must be seen in and through us. Sanctification is Christ.

All Things Are OUT FROM God

The same principle holds for all that is of God. We are earthen vessels. He is the Treasure. As Paul also said to the Corinthians:

Therefore, if any man [be] in Christ, [he is] a new creature: old things are passed away; behold, all things are become new. And all things [are out] of God, (II Cor. 5:17-18)

Paul is telling us that if we are in Christ — if Christ is in us — if we are joined to the Lord in spirit — then that spiritual union constitutes the new creation.

But the next phrase, "old things are passed away," is a misleading translation. It actually reads, "old things are passed over." What does that mean? It means that nothing of the old man in Adam — the natural man — is incorporated into the new creation. Of course not. We are joined to the Lord in spirit — and not in psyche or body, which are, "old things" -- dimensions of the old creation. Those are passed over in this age — waiting for the resurrection.

Then Paul turns back his attention upon the new creation in Christ. He says, regarding this new creation: "All things are OUT FROM God." That is how the Greek reads.

That is a direct statement to the effect that ALL THINGS are IN Christ, and therefore, OUT FROM Christ, with Whom we are joined in spirit. And of course, the other side is that NOTHING of new creation is out from US; the natural man.

Now, we see nothing in this passage that would indicate that we are less than fully complete as those IN CHRIST. Indeed, the opposite is the Truth. If Christ is in us, we have all that God has to give IN HIM. ALL that is of the new creation is OUT FROM Him unto us.

We ARE complete in Christ. That is a primary Truth. We are not only completely saved — in our spirit -- but IN HIM we have received all that God has to give. In Colossians 2, Paul is warning about the lies that would tell us otherwise. And the fact is, wherever this primary Truth has been ignored, and wherever believers are blind to it, believers ADD to Christ with experiences.

Chapter 25
Shadow or Person

At this point in chapter 2, Paul brings his readers back to the basic Truth of Christ. He writes:

For in him dwells all the fullness of the Godhead bodily. And ye are complete in him. Who is the head of all principality and power: In whom also ye are circumcised with the circumcision made without hands, in putting off the body of the sins of the flesh by the circumcision of Christ: Buried with him in baptism, wherein also ye are risen with [him] through the faith of the operation of God, who hath raised him from the dead. And you, being dead in your sins and the uncircumcision of your flesh, hath he quickened together with him, having forgiven you all trespasses; Blotting out the handwriting of ordinances that was against us, which was contrary to us, and took it out of the way, nailing it to his cross; [And] having spoiled principalities and powers, he made a shew of them openly, triumphing over them in it. (Col. 2:9-15)

Paul gives a basic primer as to what Jesus Christ did for humanity, and what it means for believers. This not only solidifies the Truth that believers are COMPLETE IN CHRIST, but it is the Truth of the Redemption — which Paul summarizes — that is the basis of his next warning. He is saying, "The Redemption if finished, and you are complete in Christ, THEREFORE --

209

Let no man therefore judge you in meat, or in drink, or in respect of an holyday, or of the new moon, or of the sabbath [days]: Which are a shadow of things to come; but the body [is] of Christ. (Col. 2:16-17)

This is the warning: The Old Covenant was a SHADOW of Jesus Christ. The New Testament is the Living Christ Himself – in His people. The Redemption has sealed this. Therefore, do not allow anyone to bring you back into a relationship with a shadow.

The epistle to the Hebrews says the same thing:

For the law having a shadow of good things to come, [and] not the very image of the things. (Heb. 10:1)

There is nothing new about this warning. It is the theme of Galatians. It is the issue of law vs. grace. It is the issue as to how a human being can be made righteous enough for God. It is by the works of the law, or is it by grace?

Christians need to understand the seriousness of erring on this matter of righteousness. Paul presses this home in Galatians:

I do not frustrate the grace of God: for if righteousness [come] by the law, then Christ is dead in vain. (Gal. 2:21)

To seek to establish my righteousness through good works is actually a denial of the Redemption of Jesus Christ – a denial of the Truth of the

Redemption that Paul just shared.   It is
UNBELIEF. It is SIN. It is, "another gospel."

Righteousness

The key passage regarding this issue of
righteousness is found in Romans 3.   In that
chapter, Paul begins by discussing the complete
hopelessness of humanity:

*As it is written, There is none righteous, no,
not one: There is none that understands,
there is none that seeks after God. They are
all gone out of the way, they are together
become unprofitable; there is none that
doeth good, no, not one...Now we know that
whatever things the law says it says to
them who are under the law: that every
mouth may be stopped, and all the world
may become guilty before God. Therefore by
the deeds of the law there shall no flesh be
justified in his sight: for by the law [is] the
knowledge of sin. (Rom. 3:10-12, 19-20)*

The key point in this passage reveals the purpose
of the law: That every mouth be stopped – that
our mouth be shut by the law regarding our own
righteousness – and that our real condition of
spiritual death be revealed.   Contrast this over
and against the deception of legalism against
which Paul is warning: That by keeping the law
we can make ourselves righteous.

What we see in this passage is that if we allow
the law to fulfill the purpose of God, we will be
left exposed for who we are before the Lord. We
will have nothing we can present about ourselves

to God.   But this is actually the best thing possible. Why? Because it is the TRUTH.   And we can then joyfully fall to our knees and say, "By your grace, Oh Lord!"

That is where Paul leads us next. He gives us the solution for our complete lack of righteousness; for our completely lost condition. He writes:

But now the righteousness of God apart from the law is manifested, being witnessed by the law and the prophets; Even the righteousness of God which is by faith of Jesus Christ unto all and upon all them that believe. (Rom. 3:21-22)

The righteousness of God is, "apart," from the law. What does that mean? The Greek denotes a great chasm — the righteousness of God is separated from the works of the law like a great chasm. In other words, the righteousness of God is complete independent of anything having to do with works.

We will not understand the need for the righteousness of God — which has nothing to do with works — unless we realize that what is wrong with humanity is NOT found in what we do, or don't do. What is wrong with us is found in what we ARE — indeed, what we are unto God. We have nothing about us — nothing about our nature — which is able to become one with God.

Because the problem is what we ARE, there is nothing about us that we can present to God. There is nothing about us in which we can put our faith.   And certainly, there is nothing we can DO to change what we ARE. That leaves us at the mercy of the grace of God — which is a wonderful place to be.

Justification by Faith

The Christian doctrine of, "justification by faith," states that if we put our faith in Jesus Christ that God will impute our sin to Him, and will impute to us His righteousness. This is a great explanation of how God is able to LEGALLY and MORALLY justify the sinner because of Jesus Christ. But it does not go far enough — it does not go as far as Paul the apostle takes it. Is our righteousness only a LEGAL one? Are we merely saved LEGALLY?

Certainly, if we believe, God does IMPUTE to us the righteousness of Jesus Christ. But more importantly, if we believe, God IMPARTS to us Jesus Christ Himself. Indeed, it is because God has imparted to us Christ — that Christ is in us -- that God is able to declare us righteous and be telling the Truth: Christ IS our righteousness, and thus, we are the righteousness of God IN HIM.

Jesus Christ is the living righteousness that is a chasm apart from the law. He is given to us by grace — we are joined to Him in spirit solely, "by grace through faith." Indeed, the believer has NO OTHER righteousness.

Note that we are NOT given a righteousness of our own. No. We remain as naked as Adam. But when we abide in Christ, He is our righteousness

– this is not only legally imputed, but spiritually imparted.

> **But of him are ye in Christ Jesus, who of God _is made unto us_ wisdom, and righteousness, and sanctification, and redemption: That, according as it is written, He that glories, let him glory in the Lord. (I Cor. 1:30-31)**

Passages like this one from I Cor. 1 state outright that Jesus Christ is our righteousness. But it would seem that most of us pass these verses over and never quite grasp the meaning. We are being told that all the glory for what the believer has become belongs to Jesus Christ – Christ in us IS our wisdom, righteousness, sanctification, and redemption. HE IS. Contrast that over and against what most of us have thought: That BECAUSE of what Jesus did, God makes US righteous, etc.

This error leads to much trouble. If you think that God has made YOU righteous then you are going to have to face the fact that you don't seem to be righteous at all. What are you going to do with   that? Some   get   under condemnation. Others get under whatever law they think will make them righteous like they should be. Even others despair and doubt their Christianity. But such trouble goes back to a wrong premise: We have not seen the separation of soul from spirit. We have not seen the distinction between Christ in us and our union with Him – the distinction between that and our natural man. So we read Bible verses that are talking about the new creation in Christ and look for evidence of them being fulfilled in our natural man. We will never find it.

Our natural man is supposed to come under Jesus as Lord – to come under the government of our union with Christ. But what this means is that the natural man is merely the place of EFFECT, but not the SOURCE. Christ in us is our righteousness and the effect of this will be seen in natural man. But our natural man is not the source. Christ is the source of all.

Jesus Christ is our righteousness, and the only righteousness we will ever have. But this means our righteousness in Christ is eternal, unchangeable, and not dependent upon our works. We are righteous in Christ because of HIMSELF – and in Him it is finished.

What this also means is that when we put our faith in Jesus Christ and are born from above, we are made one with Righteousness Himself. He is the source. There will be many effects IN US. But all the glory goes to Him. God is able to then tell the Truth: Declare us righteous, and impute to us a legal righteousness – because Christ Himself is in us, and we are one with Him.

Faith

Faith is not just a matter of believing I am righteous because of Christ – that certainly is an essential – but there is more. Faith is also a matter of depending upon Christ AS my righteousness – to be my righteousness continually – I depend upon Christ as my very life.

Of course, this matters when we sin — when we sin we must keep our faith in Christ as our living righteousness. Indeed, if Christ is our righteousness then there is no possibility that our sin can undo or defeat that fact. His redemption work is finished. We cannot, and need not, finish it. Neither can we add to it, or subtract from it through sin. This is why Romans 8:1 is able to say, "There is now NO condemnation for those in Christ Jesus."

I am only justified before God because of Jesus Christ. There is absolutely nothing that I contribute to justification. I am simply told I must believe and stand by faith in this great reality through Christ.

It is Finished

Paul issues us the warning that we must NOT allow anyone to judge us because we do not keep certain rules and laws. Why? Because God does not judge us on that basis. We are not made righteous on any other basis except that Jesus Christ in us is our righteousness. We are to walk with this Living Christ. We are not to walk in, "another gospel," with, "another Jesus," who is merely a shadow.

Chapter 26
Holding to the Head

Paul's fourth and final warning in Colossians 2:

Let no man beguile you of your reward in a voluntary humility and worshipping of angels, intruding into those things which he hath not seen, vainly puffed up by his fleshly mind, And not holding the Head, from which all the body by joints and bands having nourishment ministered, and knit together, increases with the increase of God. Wherefore if ye be dead with Christ from the rudiments of the world, why, as though living in the world, are ye subject to ordinances, (Touch not; taste not; handle not; Which all are to perish with the using;) after the commandments and doctrines of men? Which things have indeed a shew of wisdom in will worship, and humility, and neglecting of the body; not in any honor to the satisfying of the flesh. (Col. 2:18-23)

There are some points in this warning that are similar to the others we have seen. But the first point is unique to this passage. He speaks of a, "voluntary humility" – the Greek means, "rejoicing in humility," and the, worshipping of angels." He contrasts this over and against, "holding to the Head."

The word here for, "angels," is, "messenger" -- and at least in principle it could apply to ministers – to those who claim to be a messenger of God.

217

Either way, Paul is warning against the worship —
which would include submission to, the exaltation
of, and a preoccupation with, those who claim to
be messengers sent from God.

Link this up with the fact that in the first chapters
of the book of Revelation Jesus addresses His
comments — not directly to the churches -- but to,
"the angels," of the various churches.   Yet His
comments are certainly not directed to the spirit
beings that are angels.   His comments apply to
the people in those churches.   So anyway you
want to look at it, where there is a spiritual
messenger called an angel, there are people —
especially leaders of churches — involved.

The point is this: Paul is warning against a
religious deception that requires the worship of
leadership.   The practical outworking of this,
"worship," would be to look to church leadership
as not only God's messenger — but to look to
leadership as your personal MEDIATOR unto God.
In other words, God's relationship with you must
flow down from God through the leadership to
you, and it must flow out from you through that
leadership up to God. This is a direct denial of
Jesus Christ as sole Mediator between God and
ourselves through Jesus Christ. It is also a denial
that believers are already one in spirit with
Christ.

From that false premise, "submission," to these
leaders and authorities will automatically emerge.
You will be taught that you must SUBMIT to such
leadership — in order to be submissive to God
Himself. You must be, "under the authority," of
such leadership in order to be, "under the

authority," of God Himself. To refuse to submit to this authority is rebellion against God Himself. But to submit to them will not only keep you in God's will and in God's grace – but it will make you humble.

Likewise, this teaching falsely claims to be the key to Christian unity. If everyone submits to a leader, it is said that this is unity in Christ. If anyone refuses to submit, then they are rebellious -- and bringing division. But submitting to leadership never brings unity in Christ. Only if each individual, "holds to the Head," is there unity with others who, "hold to the Head."

Herein we see how handing over one's will to leadership can deceive a person into believing they are staying humble – this is the, "rejoicing in humility," that Paul mentions. Every one of us knows that we have a rebellious streak and so teachings like this offer us freedom from that – just submit to leadership and you will escape rebellion and keep humble. You will avoid God's curse and stay in His blessing.

The infallibility of the pope is an example of it. More recently, "The Shepherding Movement," of the early 1970's taught this, as does heretic Bill Gothard. This evil teaching, as noted, is a direct denial that believers have a personal, individual, one on one relationship with God -- ONLY through His Son, Jesus Christ. But the real damage is that believers are stripped of their personal relationship with Jesus Christ -- and must consult and get approval from their authority even on personal decisions.

This is, of course, Satanic. It is Satanic because it is a denial of the Truth of Christ in the individual — a denial of Christ as the only Mediator for each individual — a denial of the faithfulness of Christ in the life of the individual. And yet this heresy has been around since the beginning — people wanting to control others, all in the name of Christ.

Paul says the solution to this is for each believer to HOLD to the HEAD. Of course. Jesus Christ is the personal HEAD of each believer — not a church leader.

Unity in the Body of Christ

In this warning from Paul, he says that the reason such deception finds a place in the body of Christ is because believers do not, "hold to the Head." Most probably do not know what that means because they don't personally KNOW the Head, Jesus Christ. So through ignorance they are able to be deceived. And there is some unbelief that is usually involved — because people think they can produce humility in themselves by something they do or don't do. It is all of, "another gospel."

But Paul gets right to the core. He tells us, not only the problem, but gives the solution. Believers must personally and individually, HOLD TO THE HEAD. That is the key to our personal Christianity, and it is the key to unity in the Body of Christ:

*...**not holding the Head, from which all the body by joints and bands having***

220

nourishment ministered, and knit together, increases with the increase of God.

TRUE unity is only possible in the Person, Jesus Christ. But what does that mean? It means that if I am a partaker of Christ – in communion with Him – and you are a partaker of Christ – in communion with Him – then we are partakers of each other – in communion with each other. That is the basis of unity. Of course, it still has to be LIVED OUT. But unity through submission to even the best church authority we could find is never the means of unity in Christ – and any leadership that is preaching the Truth will TELL YOU SO.

Many groups believe that unity is achieved from the, "top down," that is, unity is imposed through law, or legislated from the top down through a statement of faith. Even worse, unity is often not in the Person of Jesus Christ, but in doctrines and facts about Him. The individual's communion with Christ thus becomes, not the basis of unity, but an issue that isn't even considered at all.

We need to be clear on this matter: It does not matter how much you, "submit," to authority, nor, "sign off," on a statement of faith, or intellectually agree with doctrines – it does not matter how much you hop aboard the "band wagon" of your local church or a ministry – it does not matter how much verbal assent you give, or how much physical service you contribute – your unity with other members of the Body of Christ is directly dependent upon your personal and individual communion with Christ Himself.

The Purpose of Ministry

The direct purpose of ministry is NOT unity. No. Unity is supposed to be a RESULT. The direct purpose of ministry is edification in Christ -- personally and individually. And if this is happening in the individuals in the Body, then the RESULT will be the Body as a whole operating in unity.

And he gave some, apostles; and some, prophets; and some, evangelists; and some, pastors and teachers; for the perfecting of the saints, for the work of the ministry, for the edifying of the body of Christ: till we all come in the unity of the faith, and of the knowledge of the Son of God, unto a perfect man, unto the measure of the stature of the fullness of Christ: (Eph. 4:13)

Christ in you, the hope of glory, whom we preach, warning every man, and teaching every man in all wisdom; that we may present every man perfect in Christ Jesus. (Col. 1:27-28)

The fact is, if individuals in the Body are being built up in Christ, then the Body as a whole is being built up in Christ, and in turn, is able to continue to build up the individuals, etc. This is the process of growth. It is silly to imagine that an individual could grow in Christ by simply being physically present in a Body of believers – because at some point, even if that Body is spiritually healthy, that person must individually come to know Christ in an inward way for themselves. You cannot know Christ by proxy. You cannot, "absorb," Christ through some spiritual process of osmosis. You have to personally have Christ revealed IN YOU, and come into a personal realization of Him. The ministry of the Body is supposed to be unto this end.

The Vine and the Branches

The picture that Jesus gave of Himself as the Vine and we as the branches illustrates this Truth. Jesus said, "I am the Vine, and you are the branches…..abide in ME." He did NOT say that we were to abide in EACH OTHER – no -- He said that communion among branches is the result of first abiding in Him. It is secondary. EACH branch must first abide in the Vine for themselves – the life of each branch is found only in the Vine. Nothing else is possible without this foundational communion between the branch and the Vine; between ourselves and Jesus Christ.

Jesus also said, "If a branch is not abiding in the Vine it will die." He did not say, "If a branch is not abiding in the other branches, it will die." This is not to minimize the value of fellowship among believers. But imagine if the branches were all abiding in each other, but not in the Vine. They would all die.

Do we realize that unity – let us continue in this picture of the Vine and the branches – do we realize that a false Christian unity among branches is possible simply if the branches are abiding in EACH OTHER? Sure. Even if NONE of those branches are abiding in the Vine, but abiding in each other, there will be a show of unity. You can have groups of professing

223

Christians in full agreement and in full communion with each other – but their agreement is in ERROR; their communion is not in Christ, but in something instead of Christ. They will have unity. But it will NOT be unity in Christ. It will be unity is something instead of Christ.

What is the core problem here? Not unity. They have unity. Cults have unity. Boy, do they have unity. But their unity is not in Christ. It is unity, yes, in a list of false teaching. But really, their unity is in their blindness and unbelief – regardless of the false teaching that emerges. And you do not need to be in an official cult to have such false unity. You could have a group of Christian people all of whom are under the same deception and the same spirit of unbelief – they could actually be celebrating their unity – but none of it is in Christ.

How many realize that unity among any group of people can achieve much? How about Nazi Germany? They had great unity – they achieved much evil. Thus, as far as proving it is good, or the Truth, or that God is in it, UNITY MEANS NOTHING. In fact, it is the will of God to utterly and completely destroy all unity that is not in His Son, Jesus Christ.

Jesus Christ said:

Think not that I am come to send peace on earth: I came not to send peace, but a sword. For I am come to set a man at variance against his father, and the daughter against her mother, and the daughter in law against her mother in

224

law. And a man's foes shall be they of his own household. (Matt. 10:34-36)

Jesus Christ is clearly stating that there is only ONE UNITY that is of God — it is unity IN THE SON. Not just unity in doctrines or facts about Jesus. That is good. But true unity is more. It is a unity that is the result of individuals HOLDING TO THE HEAD — it is the result of individuals who share in common the Person of Jesus Christ. If Jesus Christ is in me, He is to BE MY LIFE. If Jesus Christ is in you, He is to BE YOUR LIFE. Then we are EACH partakers of Christ. But that makes us partakers of each other; that means we are in communion with each other. This is communion IN CHRIST.

Every other unity is outside of God's will, and ultimately destructive. Jesus said, "I am come"…..to bring division to all of these other kinds of unity; "I am come," to destroy unity in all else by MYSELF. Notice the words, "I am come." If Jesus COMES to dwell in a person, or if the Truth and life of Jesus is introduced into a group, that is a great thing. But one of the first things Jesus Christ does when, "He comes," is to break apart all that is not of Himself. He will break apart all unity that is not in Himself so that, once this is broken, there can come to pass a true unity in Himself.

Jesus does not come to affirm the status quo. He IS the Truth. He IS the Light. And Truth and Light will at first result in JUDGMENT of all that is not of Christ. Do we want revival? This will be the first step. But it is good. It is redemptive. And it is the ONLY possibility if we

225

want to walk with, and have unity, in Jesus Christ.

So again, we see this Truth: The ministry of the Body of Christ is to edify each other in Christ. God wants to use ministry as a vehicle by which individuals can personally come to know and realize Jesus Christ for themselves. But if individuals are growing in Christ, then the Body as a whole is growing in Christ, and can, in turn, help the individuals grow.

The foundation of Christianity is, "Christ in YOU." Christ dwells in His Body — not in some unidentifiable, nebulous way, but Christ dwells in His Body by dwelling in the members of His Body, individually and personally. This is the basis of unity: We are all one IN JESUS CHRIST — the "all" becomes "the one" only because the "we" — the individuals -- are first IN CHRIST personally. The Body of Christ is mature only to the degree that, "each person is mature in Christ."

One Mediator

One of the best verses in the Bible that describes God's will for unity is found in I Timothy:

> *For there is one God, and one mediator between God and men, the man Christ Jesus. (I Tim. 2:5)*

A MEDIATOR is the One through Whom we go to connect to another. Jesus Christ is the One through Whom we go to connect to God. But the better way to say it is that Jesus Christ in us is the means through Whom we abide in the Father. Thus, if we abide in Christ – if we live in Him and out from Him – we are abiding in the Father. This is COMMUNION. Be a partaker of Christ and you are a partaker of the Father.

Now you will note: There is only ONE Mediator between EACH person and God – Jesus Christ. What this means is that you are not required, indeed, you cannot, and must not, try to abide in God through any other mediator. You cannot abide in Christ, or in God, through any part of the BODY of Christ. Mechanically, you are not, "plugged into," God or Christ because you are, "plugged into," a church, a leader, or because you are first in the Body of Christ. No. That is backwards. You are, "plugged into," God through Christ alone – personally and individually. And then, if you are in Christ, you are, so to speak, "plugged into," his church.

Our VERTICAL relationship with God, personally and individually, comes first, and will govern all HORIZONTAL relationships with other Christians. It is going to do that even if we don't realize it. Walk with Christ in spirit and in Truth and this will result in a walk with other Christians in spirit and in Truth. But try to walk with other Christians in spirit and in Truth first, to keep some law or principle of submission to authority or some principle of unity, and you will ALL end up in error. You will not be having Jesus Christ in common – not be in communion with Christ – but you will have in common just a bunch of religion.

How many see how essential it is for us to come into a personal realization of Jesus Christ? To have Christ revealed WITHIN us? This not only governs all else, but the ministry of the Body is supposed to be unto that end. Thus, the lack of knowing Jesus Christ in this way is the reason why there is no real unity in the Body of Christ. If we do not personally know Him, there can be no basis for unity that is supposed to be IN HIM.

Jesus Christ is the sole Mediator unto God. For you and I, it means that we each have personal and individual access to God through Him. Sure. He dwells in us. We don't have to go through anyone else or through any group. This is Christianity: Christ in YOU. Jesus having come to dwell in YOU.

But the anointing which ye have received of him abides in you, and ye need not that any man teach you: but as the same anointing teaches you of all things, and is truth, and is no lie, and even as it hath taught you, ye shall abide in him. (I John 2:27)

If we come into a personal knowledge of Jesus Christ, it is not going to result in any kind of prideful, superior attitude. To the contrary, we are going to desire to fellowship with other Christians – and even if God does not make that possible, the desire will be there. It would seem that today God is not on a campaign to create many local gatherings of Christian people who display great unity. Rather, many are scattered. But there is UNITY IN SPIRIT.

228

NT leadership is going to teach us exactly what John is teaching us in the above passage – that the Jesus Christ who dwells in us is our life, our Truth, and our teacher. The goal of all true ministry that is of God will be to teach this to individuals – and be a vehicle unto that end. This will serve, not only God's purpose in individuals, but it will keep the unity of the Body of Christ.

Chapter 27
Prayer and Intercession for the Saints

For a believer, prayer and intercession ought to be a regular part of life in Christ. We can pray for ourselves, of course, but prayer and intercession for others is a foundational part of ministry.

When we think of ministry, we tend to think of preaching or teaching. But many are not called to preach or teach. Yet ALL are called to pray and intercede for others. Indeed, if we are growing in Christ, prayer and intercession will likewise grow to occupy more of our attention

What is Intercession?

Intercession is not a matter of begging God to do something we think is needed. Neither is it a matter of basing our faith on our ability to reach God through prayer. Rather, to intercede, I must put myself aside. Intercession is a matter of being apprehended by God to stand with HIM for HIS will and HIS purpose -- regarding the one for whom you intercede, or regarding the situation in question. Intercession is for God's will, His way, in His time -- regardless of cost.

In the NT Greek, the word for "intercession" carries the meaning, "to fall in with; to meet with" -- usually on the behalf of another. So despite the fact that Jesus, "ever lives to make intercession for the saints according to the will of God" – and obviously doesn't need our help -- part of fellowship with Christ is that we will, "fall in with Him; become one with Him," in interceding for others. We will have His mind and heart on these matters.

Intercession also means that we are sometimes praying for those who do not know to pray for themselves. This does not replace their responsibility to choose. Rather, intercession eventually makes choice for them clear and possible.

To stand with God for His will "no matter what" is equal to asking, "Thy kingdom come, Thy will be done, on earth as it is in heaven." How is God's will done in heaven? Fully. That is what we are seeking when we stand with God in His purpose.

Intercession is Fellowship

If I am in fellowship with Jesus Christ, then the more I grow in Christ, the more that my fellowship with Christ will increase. This will mean that I will be growing to be one with HIS interests. My heart will belong to Him and grow to reflect His heart. This will not necessarily be something I can document. It is the outcome of coming into an inward realization of Jesus Christ.

Paul referred to what he called, "the fellowship of His sufferings." (Phil. 3:9) Note that, "fellowship," means, "a having in common." Therefore, "the fellowship of His sufferings," means that we will grow to suffer WITH Christ in what He is suffering. We will not only care about what He cares about, but there is actually BE suffering. There will be a burden. It will affect us. This will most certainly result in INTERCESSION.

What this leads us to see is that intercession is not merely something we DO. Rather, intercession emerges from what we are – or better said – intercession emerges from who Christ is IN US. Another way to say this is this: Because Jesus Christ, "ever lives to make intercession for the saints" (Heb. 7:25), then this is what He will be doing if He lives IN US. And we will eventually find ourselves being caught up together with Him into His intercession.

Prayer or Intercession

Real intercession is actually a dimension of Jesus Christ living in and through us. We are simply caught up in HIS intercession for the saints, or anyone else. This should not be surprising because believers are members of His Body. That means that we are extensions of Him. Of course, I am talking about what God wants us to be. Today few are extensions of Jesus Christ. Despite being members of His Body, today many are doing their own thing. Fellowship in Christ is today an unknown – replaced by religious substitutes. Therefore real intercession is also a relative unknown.

Intercession is not the same as general prayer. In prayer, we are free to bring our requests before the Lord; to ask Him; to seek Him. But with intercession we are apprehended by Christ to stand with Him for HIS will, HIS interests – no matter what it takes. We are being used by Jesus Christ – as extension of Him; as members of Christ -- to, "stand in the gap,"

(Ezek. 22:30) for those who cannot pray, or don't know to pray, for themselves.

The fact is, the more we grow in Christ, the more we will stand with Him for His will and interests even in our OWN requests. We will not want to settle for anything less that God's highest. This is always the outcome of knowing and believing Him.

There is simply no way to grow in Jesus Christ without eventually, to one extent or another, being caught up into the fellowship of His sufferings – without being caught up in intercession. In short, intercession will become part of life in Christ. Because He lives to intercede, we will live in Him to intercede.

Intercession in the Spirit

Intercession is spiritual. But because it is spiritual, we will often not know exactly why we are interceding, nor will we necessarily see results in ways that we might expect. There are spiritual forces and powers that are involved. We are standing IN CHRIST and WITH CHRIST for His will and victory.

It only makes sense that there are going to be times when we are caught up into something of God that we don't quite understand. How could we possibly know what is going on – especially when many issues are in the realm of spiritual things? That is why intercession is not something WE initiate. No. Jesus initiates it. Left to ourselves we would not know what to pray or how to deal with a situation in prayer. It would be beyond us. But the Bible states that Jesus Christ, our intercessor and High Priest, takes the initiative to, by His spirit, "make intercession for the saints according to the will of God." (see Romans 8:26-27) Well, we have Christ in us by the means of the Holy Spirit. Thus, when He begins to intercede we can be caught up in it.

Many people have been taught that the Holy Spirit, and not Jesus, is our intercessor. But this is not correct. I realize that some of the English wording out of the passage from Romans 8 might leave that impression. But if you read passages like Romans 8:9-13 you will see that not only does Christ dwell in us by the spirit of God, but these are used interchangeably. Indeed, the fact remains that we have only ONE High Priest, and a primary function of the High Priest was intercession. The absolutely weight of scripture shows Jesus as our intercessor. In fact, it show that Jesus does not merely intercede as a thing to DO. Rather, the presence of Christ in us is a living intercession – He is our living Mediator unto God. Thus, it is Jesus Christ, our High Priest, who, "ever lives to make intercession for us" – He does this BY the spirit of God.

So what we see is that intercession is not so much an ASKING of God to do something – although this might be included. Rather, it is a standing WITH Christ for what HE already wants to do – He has apprehended us for this intercession -- even though we might not know exactly what is at stake.

As stated earlier, Christ does not need our help. But we will forever be one with Him and in fellowship with Him. And He lives to intercede. Thus, intercession – standing with Christ at all cost – comes with the territory of being ONE with Jesus Christ.

The Working of God's Will

God has a WILL. That should hardly be questioned. But if God does have a will then, by definition, He wants to bring to pass His will – He wants to bring to pass His will because IT IS His will. God is not confused about what He wants. He is not making it up as He goes along. God's will is a perfect will and never changes.

If God's will was nothing more than circumstances that pleased Him there would be little need for intercession. But the primary will of God is that people come into an inward realization and fellowship with His Son. This is unto the end that His Body as a whole be an expression of Jesus Christ as Lord. Thus, intercession has THIS purpose of God at its core.

This primary purpose of God does not exclude the intervention and help of God on other matters. But everything God does in this age is unto that end. If people would come into an inward realization of Jesus Christ many other issues would be resolved as the outcome of living in Christ.

Intercession will often work towards opening the eyes of a spiritually blind person. A person must first realize they are blind – and this, in itself, equals a seeing. But in order to open the eyes of a spiritually blind person God must begin with

235

them right where they are — blind, ignorant, self-righteousness, or living in the sin of unbelief. Perhaps they are not even saved. If you examine this, there is NO solution. Logic, intellectual arguments, and emotional reactions cannot give sight to the blind. You cannot document how a spiritually blind person comes to see enough to turn to Christ. It is one of the miracles of intercession.

You will note that God does not force anyone to turn to Christ. He does not force anyone to be free. Usually what He does is open their eyes — open their eyes to their condition, and open their eyes to Jesus Christ. He brings them to the place where freedom is possible. But at some point along the way, they must choose. Intercession makes this choice possible -- where it was not possible through human effort. As you can see, there is more involved here than what can be accounted for — except that it is of God.

Many people are not aware of their condition. Perhaps they presently cannot or even will not pray for themselves — and if they do, it will be prayer that is not according to the will of God. Therefore, God will apprehend someone else to intercede on his or her behalf.

Again — such an intercession of one person on the behalf of another is NOT a matter of pleading with God for their salvation, or for their freedom. No. That would be absurd — for how could we possibly desire freedom for another person more than God desires it? Is God a God that must be nagged and begged for help? No. The point here is that if God has apprehended us for intercession it was neither our choice nor their choice. It was God's choice. And neither have we been apprehended by God to beg Him to do what He already wants to do. No. Again – we have been caught up into God's interests for a person. We are apprehended by God to stand WITH HIM on behalf of that person.

Certainly God doesn't need our help. Therefore, if we are apprehended by God for intercession we can be sure that it is not only for the benefit of the person in question, but it is likewise for our benefit. It is an opportunity to LEARN CHRIST – and to actually experience, "the fellowship of His sufferings," and to experience Christ Himself. For as mentioned earlier, intercession is not merely something we DO. It is the outcome of who Jesus Christ is IN US – and of our spiritual union with Him.

Now, when we are caught up with Christ in intercession, it should not be surprising if it seems as if NOTHING is happening for quite some time. This is because the real battle and the real foundation of change is found in the spiritual realm. God must take a person right where they are, in darkness or even unbelief, and before He can begin to show them the Truth, He must plow away at some core issues. Often God will bring people to the end of themselves – this might necessitate that they go on and on until they see that the way they are living is all futile.

There are also times when God must allow certain restrictive conditions to persist because He knows that if He just all of a sudden set a person free that they would have no anchor. They could easily fall into something worse. It is one thing for a person to see that something is wrong. It is another to see the right. It is one thing to be free from something bad. But it is another to be free TO something good. The point is, God won't usually set a person free from the terrible spiritual condition they are in presently until He knows that they do see enough to be anchored in Jesus Christ.

And so we should not be discouraged if we do not see, "results," from our intercession. It is not our responsibility to judge that. It is our responsibility, if God has apprehended us for intercession, to stand with God on behalf of the person, or the situation in question. Again – this is, at the core, a spiritual issue and battle.

If God has a will, and He has caught us up into fellowship with Him for that will – through intercession – then we can be sure that if we stand with God that His will cannot fail. It must come to pass – even if people refuse it once it does come to pass. Intercession is our participation in the will of God.

Another thing we see in this Truth of intercession is that the will of God does not come to pass by simply, "confessing it." We cannot go around, "speaking victory," into people's lives. That has become popular, but is absurd. Rather than, "speak victory," into people's lives, we ought to realize that if they are a believer, Jesus Christ is ALREADY in them. Victory is not a THING God gives people. It is not something that is separate from the Person of Christ. No. All victory is IN

Christ. This is why intercession will have as a primary goal that people's eyes be opened to the One who is interceding for them. Faith in Christ is the victory.

"He ever lives to make intercession." We might even say, "He ever lives to BE our intercession." Does God answer the prayers of His Son? Well, if we are caught up in intercession with Jesus Christ, then we are praying and standing WITH HIM. God will answer. In short, Jesus does not intercede only to fail. That for which Jesus intercedes WILL come to pass – in God's time, God's way, and unto His glory. Even if every man be false, God will be true.

Warfare

All through the Bible, whether it is in type and shadow, or directly, Christians are said to be engaged in a great WARFARE. This is certainly true with regards to prayer and intercession.

But why? Hasn't Jesus won all victory? So how can intercession add to a FINSHED victory? It cannot. Intercession adds NOTHING. Rather, intercession is a standing by faith – against all that is contrary – IN the finished victory of Jesus Christ. In other words, rather than ADD to the victory of Christ, intercession brings people INTO that victory; under Christ as Lord.

This often requires spiritual warfare. But spiritual warfare is not a matter of believers attacking the enemy. Intercession is not a matter of you and I mustering up out of ourselves some kind of spiritual stamina that can withstand all of the enemies of God. No. It is a matter of FAITH – of standing in Christ – in a victory finished. But standing against what? Well, if we are to stand by faith, then we are standing against UNBELIEF.

Unbelief is the real goal of the enemy. So don't think of standing with Christ in intercession in terms of demons or people openly trying to attack you – or attacking a person for whom you are interceding. That could happen -- but that is not usually the form taken by the spiritual forces that are hostile to the Lord. What Satan really wants to do is subtlety bring people into UNBELIEF. In other words, if the victory of Jesus Christ is truly finished, then the question is whether we will believe or not believe. If we believe, His victory will become ours. If we don't – we are in unbelief -- and then there can be no victory. That is why unbelief is the goal of the enemy.

So often believers get together and pray for each other for things like deliverance, or for some special touch from God that will supposedly cure what ails them. I've heard prayers for deliverance from unforgiveness, etc. But usually these prayers are based in error or misunderstanding. If we want to pray for deliverance, what we need deliverance from is UNBELIEF. Or blindness. Get free of unbelief and the result will be that you will BELIEVE – and this faith will bring you into contact with the Person who is our finished victory.

The only power that the enemy continues to have in the life of the believer is that of DECEPTION. If he can deceive us – get us onto a wrong basis − cast doubt between the Lord and ourselves − then he can destroy God's work. We must therefore stand by faith, not only for ourselves, but on behalf of any person for whom we are interceding against unbelief.

If we will ask God to do whatever it takes to bring us into the fullness of Christ, we are praying according to His will. This is how we begin to lose our lives to Him at the Cross. And if we go on with the Lord, carrying our cross, He will eventually apprehend us into a fellowship of His sufferings through intercession.

Intercession for the saints is the outcome of fellowship with Christ, but also the outcome of fellowship with other members of His body. It is not a duty. It is a living result of Christ in us, and of being members one of another. Through this ministry, God will accomplish His eternal purposes in the Body of Christ.

Chapter 28
Other Warnings

The gospels are a narrative of the life and times of Jesus Christ. They are a written revelation of His identity as the only begotten Son of God -- become man. They tell us the story of His birth, life, death, resurrection and ascension. They also contain all of His teachings and miraculous works. But within these gospels we also find a continual warfare. Jesus is attacked on all sides by Satan, and by those whom Satan could use, namely the Pharisees and Jewish leaders of His day. God had these exchanges written within His Word to expose the methods of the enemy, as well as to show us the answers found in Christ.

Much the same could be said about the book of Acts. It is a narrative rather than a doctrinal work. But again – within it we have principals established as to God's mind and purpose for His people. And we also have Satan trying to destroy it.

The epistles ARE doctrinal in nature. In fact, if we were to gather up the epistles and offer a description of what they are, we could say that the epistles are an explanation of what Christianity IS. Each of them is based upon the great Truth of, "Christ in us, the hope of glory." Each of them contains teaching as to what Christ in us means, how to experience Him, and what God has done, and is doing, and will do, through Him. And each of them addresses various attempts by the enemy – within the churches themselves – to seduce believers away – through deception -- from Christ into something or someone less.

If the epistles are an explanation of what Jesus Christ in us means – and how to live in Him as our life – then this would obviously be the target of the enemy. The enemy would seek to REDEFINE the reality of Christ within. He would seek to create and offer an alternative Christianity.

We have already seen the warnings of the apostle Paul in his epistle to the Colossians. His warnings are all based upon the Truth of, "Christ in you, the hope of glory," and, "Christ, Who is our life." i.e., CHRIST IS ALL. Thus, it is not surprising that we find similar warnings based upon the very same foundational Truth in scripture. One of the most important is given by the apostle John:

Beloved, believe not every spirit, but try the spirits whether they are of God: because many false prophets are gone out into the world. Hereby know ye the Spirit of God: Every spirit that confesses that Jesus Christ is come in the flesh is of God: And every spirit that confesses not that Jesus Christ is come in the flesh is not of God: and this is that [spirit] of antichrist, whereof ye have heard that it should come; and even now already is it in the world. (I John 4:1-3)

This passage has been almost universally ignored by the church for two thousand years. In fact, it has been so redefined and misapplied that few believers take it seriously. Most think that it applies only to a first century heresy.

Let's ask: Did God give warnings and tests in His inspired Word that applied only to Christians two thousand years ago? Before the Bible was even written or available in any widespread sense? Or can we be sure that what God is telling us applies for the entire church age?

In John's day, Gnosticism was invading the church. This warning was against that heresy. But do we realize that the core, spiritual deception of Gnosticism is alive and well today -- under other names, movements, and manifestations? Sure. The lies of the enemy are ultimately lies about the Person of Jesus Christ. Thus, no matter the manifestation, the LIE is still there – in principle. The lies of the enemy misrepresent the Person of Jesus Christ, and more specifically, distort what Christianity IS – distort the foundation of CHRIST IN YOU. Once people are deceived regarding that Truth, everything else is going to be amiss.

Gnosticism taught that Jesus did not really become a flesh and blood human being. Rather, He just appeared as one. But notice the ramifications of this lie: There is NO redemption for human beings. And extending from that it would be impossible for Jesus Christ to dwell within human beings.

If Jesus were not human then human beings could not become one with Him in resurrection union. And that negates salvation itself, because it is through resurrection union that Jesus Christ

244

dwells within us as OUR LIFE. Thus, Christianity itself is denied through redefinition – and we have, "another Jesus; another gospel."

Test the Spirits

Let's look at the words of John. He warns us to, "test the spirits." How many congregations actually take this command seriously? What makes this all the more precarious is that none of us can really, "test the spirits," unless we have a standard against which to test. But John gives us that standard. What does he write?

He says, "Every spirit that confesses Jesus having come in the flesh is of God." In contrast, he adds, "Every spirit that confesses NOT that Jesus having come in the flesh is NOT of God." That spirit, John says, is, "the spirit of antichrist."

The Truth of, "Jesus having come in the flesh," is the test. This is the Truth that the spirit of God will always reveal; will always speak; will always center our lives upon. Is this not exactly the same Truth as, "Christ in you, the hope of glory?" Is it not the reality of flesh and blood human beings joined to the Lord and made one spirit with Him? Is this not speaking of the Treasure in earthen vessels? Yes. John is teaching that Jesus Christ is the One whom God SPEAKS – confesses, and reveals within believers – by His spirit. John is teaching that the core reality of Christianity is CHRIST IN BELIEVERS.

But as an aside, note something interesting: John does tell us what the spirit of God WILL confess. But he does NOT tell us what the spirit of antichrist will confess − but instead -- tells us what the spirit of antichrist will NOT confess. The spirit of antichrist will NOT confess what the spirit of God WILL confess: Jesus having come in the flesh.   In short, it does not matter what the spirit of antichrist DOES confess − because the spirit of antichrist will use any method available to blind believers to the Truth of Jesus having come in the flesh − to blind believers to the foundational Truth of CHRIST IN YOU.   And as noted, once believers are blind to Christ, everything else is going to be off the track. Christianity itself will be redefined.

John is stating that if Jesus Christ, the Son of God, did not actually become a flesh and blood human being, then He could not − through His Redemptive work − make Himself one with human beings.   There would be NO such reality as CHRIST IN BELIEVERS.   There would be no such Christianity.   All would be redefined according to another Jesus -- and another redemption.

Isn't this exactly what has happened for two thousand years, and is being continued today?

We need to get his settled: Christianity is CHRIST IN YOU, the hope of glory.   But not merely the doctrine − Christianity is the LIVING CHRIST in His people; Christ in us as OUR LIFE. Any other presentation of Christianity is ANTICHRIST.   It is just that serious.

John is not talking about a debate as to whether some sort of manifestation is of God.   He is not referring to some obscure, ancient heresy that the early church had to confront.   Rather, he is talking about the very core of the purpose and plan of God. That accounts for the strong language, and the seriousness of his tone.

We saw earlier that Jesus Christ is the WORD God is speaking. We saw that this means more than God merely talking about Jesus, or God inspiring teaching about Jesus. God speaks Jesus Christ in that He reveals Christ IN US. We are joined to the Lord at salvation and the work of the spirit of God is to reveal Christ TO us, IN us, and ultimately THROUGH us. This is what the spirit of God confesses — it is the Living Word that God speaks. The spirit of antichrist will NOT speak this — the spirit of antichrist will blind, hide, and offer substitutes for foundation of Christianity. And that is what has been accomplished for two thousand years.

A Personal Indwelling

These [things] have I written unto you concerning them that seduce you. But the anointing which ye have received of him abides in you, and ye need not that any man teach you: but as the same anointing teaches you of all things, and is truth, and is no lie, and even as it hath taught you, ye shall abide in him. (I John 2:26-27)

Note that John is writing these words, "concerning them that seduce you." It is a warning, similar to that of Paul's in Colossians 2, against the many devices of the enemy to deceive us into a false Christianity. In this passage, John brings home the essential Truth that Christianity is a personal, one-on-one relationship with Christ

247

– based upon the fact that we are personally indwelt by Christ.

It is clear that John is concerned that believers would fail to abide in Christ as their life, and as their all, and be seduced into looking unto other sources, people, movements, or leaders. He is saying, "Christ is IN YOU. He is ONE with you. Let no one tell you otherwise."

John's warning here is based upon the same Truth as the one we have just discussed about, "testing the spirits." Christianity at the core is CHRIST IN US. Be seduced away from Him and you are going to be deceived.

What we are seeing throughout the entirety of the NT is this: Jesus Christ – Jesus Christ, Who is in us – is our LIFE. He is ALL to the believer. The NT is an explanation and a revelation of this great reality.

But the NT does not merely exhort believers to hold to doctrines that teach this – although that is necessary. We MUST hold to NT doctrine. But the NT exhorts us and warns us to hold to CHRIST HIMSELF – we are exhorted to abide in the Living Christ by faith. In other words, we are to live by faith in and from out of the Living Christ who dwells within each believer. Christ is our life and we must experience Him as our life.

Chapter 29
The Unshakable Kingdom

Christianity is not a religion. It is not a belief system. It is not a condition of mind or an expression of emotion. No. Christianity is CHRIST IN US. Christianity is a spiritual oneness, leading to a living experience, with God Almighty through His Son, Jesus Christ.

Jesus said, "I AM the resurrection and the LIFE." That makes Jesus Christ ALL. God has freely given believers all things in His Son. He has given NOTHING to anyone outside of Christ.

It is the purpose of God to reveal Christ TO us, and then IN us, and then through us. God intends to use the body of Christ as expressions of Christ, and extensions of Christ, in this age, but especially in the age to come.

These are unchangeable, eternal Truths. They cannot be shaken. But the fact is, ALL ELSE — everything that is not of Christ -- is going to be shaken and burnt. It is going to be burned and pass out of existence.

This ought to be GOOD news. Indeed, God has promised this very thing in the epistle to the Hebrews:

But now he hath promised, saying, Yet once more I shake not the earth only, but also heaven. And this word, Yet once more, signifies the removing of those things that are shaken, as of things that are made, that those things which cannot be shaken may remain. Wherefore we receiving a kingdom which cannot be moved, let us have grace, whereby we may serve God acceptably with reverence and godly fear: For our God is a consuming fire. (Heb. 12:26-29)

Has this shaking already happened? Impossible — because when this shaking is finished, only that which is of Christ shall remain. Is that what we see today? Nothing close. Thus, this shaking is yet to come.

This promise of a great SHAKING and BURNING is repeated using the similar picture of God as a consuming fire -- in Paul's first epistle to the Corinthians:

For another foundation can no man lay than that is laid, which is Jesus Christ. Now if any man build upon this foundation gold, silver, precious stones, wood, hay, stubble; Every man's work shall be made manifest: for the day shall declare it, because it shall be revealed by fire; and the fire shall try every man's work of what sort it is. If any man's work abide which he hath built thereupon, he shall receive a reward. If any man's work shall be burned, he shall suffer loss: but he himself shall be saved; yet so as by fire. (I Cor. 3:11-15)

Again, God has repeatedly promised that when He is finished with His purpose in this age that all that is going to remain is that which is of Christ:

That in the dispensation of the fullness of times he might gather together in one all things in Christ, both which are in heaven, and which are on earth; even in him. (Eph. 1:10)

Do we realize what this means? If ALL that will remain is that which is of Christ, then NOTHING will remain that is of man. What a fantastic promise! What a fantastic victory! What an incredible Redemption!

But do we think God is talking merely about world governments? Is that what he is going to shake and burn? No. Read again the passage from Hebrews. At one time God DID shake the earthly. And He intends to do it again. But now His promise is shake -- to the foundations -- all that is heavenly. The, "heavenly," speaks of the spiritual realm.

God is going to shake to the core all that appears to be spiritual, all that appears to be built upon Jesus Christ, or appears to be OF Christ. That means churches, denominations, ministries, and movements. But most of all, God is going to shake the personal, spiritual life of believers. God promises to SHAKE us – this will expose us and our faith for what we are. And then we will have the opportunity to turn to God and confess the Truth. But in the end, God Himself will be as a consuming fire. He will consume all that is not of Christ – so that all that will remain eternally is that which IS of Christ.

Revival

People call for revival. But do we realize that this passage is actually describing revival that is of God? Of course, it is more of a REFORMATION. But whether you call it REVIVAL or REFORMATION – it is JUDGMENT. Judgment always begins with LIGHT – it always begins with God exposing everything for what it is. That is the shaking. And then people are accountable for the choices they make. God will then bring final judgment. That is the burning.

The writer of Hebrews is, of course, speaking of a great FUTURE dealing by God, which will bring an end to this present age. But can we see that for believers such a shaking and burning is going on right now? Judgment BEGINS with the house of God. (I Peter 4:17)

This is all for our good, and for our freedom. God is dealing with us as SONS. He is keeping all of His promises in Christ.

A Personal Shaking

There are millions of professing Christian people who, right now, have a faith and a religious life in Christ, that is built of perishable materials. It is not real. It is religion.

Certainly ALL of us begin that way to a certain extent. That is why God allows trials in our lives. What is the purpose of these personal trials? Is not the purpose exactly what is stated in Hebrews -- to shake us so that only that which is of Christ remains? Is not the purpose to BURN up, through the fires of the trial, all that is temporal, so that only that which is eternal in Christ remains? Absolutely. Thus, many of God's people have experienced, in a personal way, what these passages promise.

But again, there is yet to come a more universal fulfillment of these promises of God. There is going to come a time when God shakes the core of what we today view as Christianity. He is going to shake it all -- so that the Truth about it will be exposed. Whether our faith resided upon the institutions, churches, ministries, and preachers -- or upon the person of Jesus Christ -- this will all be exposed. God is going to knock out from under us all of the religious crutches. This is going to be REAL -- and it is going to be traumatic. And in the end, it will prove to be redemptive and good.

Many people are predicting some great end-time revival that is going to sweep millions upon millions into the kingdom of God. But the Bible never says that this is going to happen. What God does promise in His Word is that before the end of the age there is going to come forth an undeniable witness to Jesus Christ. Not one person, not one movement, and not one ministry. It will be spiritual — fully wrought by God. It will reveal the Person of Jesus Christ so that all who want the real Jesus can turn.

The revelation of Jesus Christ is the light that will bring the great shaking and ultimate judgment of God. In these last days, there has not yet been a real revelation of Jesus Christ. Thus, how can there be the apostasy predicted by Paul? How can there be a falling away unless there is a revelation of Christ from which to fall? There can't be. God is going to have His witness. This will cause a great shaking and collapse of what today passes for Christianity and many will not accept it.

Serious Questions

Do we really want Jesus Christ -- and only Jesus Christ? Are we willing to allow God to do whatever it takes to bring to pass His full will and purpose in Christ? Well, look around you. What do you and I think that IS going to take? It is going to take a great shaking -- the core and foundation of this fake institution that we call Christianity is going to have to be shaken. And it will be shaken once Jesus Christ is revealed.

If we want to know what we need to be doing in these times, so that we might be ready for the great shaking, the answer is that we need to allow God to shake us NOW. God wants to establish us in Jesus Christ NOW – reveal in us His Son NOW – that Christ, and Christ alone, may be our life. And if He does -- then we will have a Rock and an anchor that is eternal.

Chapter 30
Sonship in the Son

But as many as received him, to them gave he power to become the sons of God, [even] to them that believe on his name: Which were born, not of blood, nor of the will of the flesh, nor of the will of man, but of God. (John 1:12-13)

Scripture calls Jesus Christ the FIRSTBORN. This does not mean He was, "born again," in the way in which lost sinners must become born again, but it means that through His death and resurrection He ushered a new creation of humanity — IN HIMSELF. In Christ, those who turn to Him become new creations.

For whom he did foreknow, he also did predestinate [to be] conformed to the image of his Son, that he might be the firstborn among many brethren. (Rom. 8:29)

And he is the head of the body, the church: who is the beginning, the firstborn from the dead; that in all [things] he might have the preeminence. (Col. 1:18)

Sonship in and through Jesus Christ is the plan and purpose of God for each believer. This is the result of Christ as our LIFE. It is why God is speaking in His Son. It is therefore vital that believers see the meaning of sonship.

In the Bible, to be born a child, and then to be adopted as a son, carry different meanings than our normal usage today — the Bible meanings are pulled out of that culture during that time. In that time, to be a SON was not the result of being born into a family. No. You were a child. It was only when you reached maturity and were, "adopted," that you became a SON – which is to say – you became one who could be responsible for your inheritance.

This represents God's plan for believers as sons and daughters who are to inherit all things in Christ. Being born from above makes us, "children of God." But the ultimate goal of God is that as children we would reach maturity in Christ and be able to experience and be responsible for that which is given in Him – be responsible for our eternal inheritance. When we begin to be mature, it is said that we are, "adopted," as SONS and DAUGHTERS.

But therein is a vital Truth with regards to sonship – and that Truth is this: Sonship is only in the Son. To put it another way, there is only ONE Son of God. But we can become sons and daughters IN HIM.

Contrast this over and against the false idea that Jesus is the BIG Son of God, and we are smaller sons and daughters of God, lined up beside Him. No. We are not sons and daughters of God in addition to Jesus, besides Jesus, or sort of because of Jesus. Rather, we are sons and daughters of God IN Jesus Christ.

Another way to state this Truth is to describe God's plan of inheritance – which is His plan for sons and daughters. That plan is this: The

Father, the uniquely begotten Son, and sons and daughters IN the Son.

The point is, a Christian is a human being who is joined to the Lord and made one spirit with Him. (I Cor. 6:17) We are IN CHRIST – i.e., Christ is in us – in resurrection union. This means that we have been given ALL of Christ – and thus, have been given all that is in Him. Everything that God has to give humanity is given in, and only given in, the Person of His Son.

This speaks of inheritance. There is only ONE SON who inherits all things: Jesus Christ. But because we are joined to Him we are COHEIRS with Him. This does not mean He inherits the most and we inherit less. No. What it does mean is that He inherits all, but to the extent that we are able to be responsible and faithful in our relationship to Him, we inherit and live in ALL.

So, the spiritual union of believers with Jesus Christ is the new birth – it makes us children of God. But it takes a lifetime to discover the Christ with Whom we have been joined. It takes the work of the Cross and the inward realization of Jesus if we are to experience Him. Yet as we do, there is a faithfulness that is built in us – because we see that He is faithful. And as that is built, we can be entrusted with true riches. It is at that point that, "we receive adoption as sons."

This is the meaning behind Paul's words to the Galatians:

But when the fullness of the time was come, God sent forth his Son, made of a woman,

made under the law, To redeem them that
were under the law, that we might receive
the adoption of sons. And because ye are
sons, God hath sent forth the Spirit of his
Son into your hearts, crying, Abba, Father.
Wherefore thou art no more a servant, but a
son; and if a son, then an heir of God
through Christ. (Gal. 4:4-7)

It is also why we can know that when Paul says God has, "predestined us unto the adoption," that he is not talking about any sort of predestination unto SALVATION. No. The Calvinistic doctrine of unconditional election is error. Paul is talking about being predestined unto adoption – in other words, those who are already in Christ are predestined unto God's purpose that we might be adopted as sons.

Having predestinated us unto the adoption
of children by Jesus Christ to himself,
according to the good pleasure of his will.
(Eph. 1:5)

It is the desire and purpose of God that those who are in Christ reach FULLNESS in Christ – such that they can be given responsibility as sons and daughters in Christ. Practically speaking, this means that if we grow to where Christ lives IN us, and THROUGH us, then we can be expressions and extensions of Christ.

Reigning and Ruling

Everything that God is doing in this age is unto the end that His people might be sons and daughters IN THE SON. And that from out of the

Son, those sons and daughters might grow to be expressions and extension of Jesus Christ.

This is what it means to, "reign and rule with Christ." It isn't that Jesus hands us peoples and lands over which we will rule. Rather, HE is Lord of all, but His body is intended to be expressions and extensions of Him – vehicles of administration, if you will. He is the Head and we are His body – the body is an extension of the Head, or mind.

Which he wrought in Christ, when he raised him from the dead, and set [him] at his own right hand in the heavenly [places], Far above all principality, and power, and might, and dominion, and every name that is named, not only in this world, but also in that which is to come: And hath put all [things] under his feet, and gave him [to be] the head over all [things] to the church, Which is his body, the fullness of him that fills all in all... Even when we were dead in sins, hath quickened us together with Christ, (by grace ye are saved;) And hath raised [us] up together, and made [us] sit together in heavenly [places] in Christ Jesus: That in the ages to come he might shew the exceeding riches of his grace in [his] kindness toward us through Christ Jesus. (Eph. 1:20-23, 2:5-8)

So, when we discuss God's purpose in Christ, and see that He wants us to come into an inward knowledge and realization of His Son, it is all unto this end: That we might receive adoption as SONS and DAUGHTERS. That we might become those to whom Jesus Christ can entrust true riches. That we might become extensions and expressions of Christ – yes, starting now – but unto a full release in the eternal ages. That is INHERITANCE – HE is our true spiritual inheritance.

So we see that reigning and ruling with Christ is nothing more than a matter of ministering Christ to others. Yet, not by some governmental law – but through the ministration of HIS LIFE – through His love; His Truth. Isn't this, to a limited degree, what the body of Christ is supposed to be doing in this age?

Serious Business

Can we see that the church, as a whole, has completely missed the purpose of God? What God has as His priority in this age is Truth to which the body of Christ is completely blinded.

This blindness had already begun in the first century. That is why Paul used such strong words to the Galatians. It is why he warned the Corinthians. And it is why he wrote to the Colossians – issuing four warnings as to the centrality of Jesus Christ.

Jesus Christ is ALL to the believer. He is the PERSON – THE LOGOS – that God is speaking. He is the One in Whom God has given all things. He is the uniquely begotten Son of God – and we are sons and daughters only IN HIM. To come to know Him – in an inward fashion – is the purpose of God and the ONLY means by which we can become those who receive adoption as sons.

Chapter 31
Eternal Inheritance in Christ

We have thus far seen that when we are joined to the Lord at salvation, and receive Him as our life, we become the, "born from above," children of God. We have also seen that as the children of God it is possible to reach a level of fullness in Christ – at which point the children are adopted as sons and daughters of God. Fullness in Christ implies that we can be given responsibility to be faithful TO Christ in all things – in other words, we will be faithful to Christ as we live in the inheritance that is found in Him.

What is the eternal inheritance of the saints? We find a suggestion in Ephesians:

> *That we should be to the praise of his glory, who first trusted in Christ. In whom ye also [trusted], after that ye heard the word of truth, the gospel of your salvation: in whom also after that ye believed, ye were sealed with that holy Spirit of promise, Which is the earnest of our inheritance until the redemption of the purchased possession, unto the praise of his glory. (Eph. 1:12-14)*

Take note: The Holy Spirit of promise is the, "earnest" – the word means, "down payment" – of our inheritance. But a, "down payment," on the fullness is always of the same nature and character of that fullness – indeed, it is OF the fullness; it is representative of the fullness. Gather that up and it means that the Holy Spirit of promise – which is the means by which Christ dwells in the believer in this age – is a down payment of Jesus Christ -- Who is going to be released in us at the resurrection. In short, Jesus Christ Himself IS our inheritance. God intends for humanity to fully experience all that Jesus Christ is, and all that Jesus Christ has done – unto the expression of Christ through that same humanity.

But why the term, "down payment?" Paul is simply saying that in this age, in these physical bodies, we are hindered by our natural soul man; we are limited as to our ability to experience Christ in fullness NOW. It is only at the resurrection, when we will be set free from all of those hindrances, that we will be able to fully experience all that Christ is.

Thus, we do receive ALL of Christ at salvation – we are fully joined to Him in spiritual union. (I Cor. 6:17) But we are not joined to him in physical body or in our soul man. That is why our spiritual union with Christ is likened to a down payment – there are aspects of our being that cannot yet fully experience or manifest Him in this age. But that which is a down payment – although fully received in spirit – will be fully experienced in every way starting with the resurrection. That is why Paul wrote:

Which is the earnest of our inheritance until the redemption of the purchased possession, unto the praise of his glory.

"The purchased possession," is the fullness of what God intends a human being to be in Christ.

The Hope of Glory

Christ in you, the hope of glory. (Col. 1:27)

This verse, above all other verses, proves that Jesus Christ in fullness IS the eternal inheritance of the saints. As noted, it is the will of God that we experience all that Christ IS through an eternal oneness with Him — leading to an expression of Him through us. Is this not what is is made possible by CHRIST IN US now, in this age? And is this not clearly indicated by saying that Christ in us NOW is, "the HOPE of glory?"

The word, "hope," in the NT Greek, does not mean, "maybe." Rather, it carries the meaning of CERTAINTY. Paul is saying that in this age Jesus Christ is in us — we are fully joined to the Lord in resurrection union — we are fully IN CHRIST. But Christ in us is the HOPE or CERTAINTY of a greater experience — possible only at the resurrection.

In effect, Christ in us NOW is the down payment out of which the fullness of Christ will be released THEN. Christ in us NOW is the HOPE of a greater release of glory THEN. And Paul says that this release IS our inheritance.

The Resurrection

Beloved, now are we the sons of God, and it does not yet appear what we shall be: but we know that when he shall appear, we shall be like him; for we shall see him as he is. (1 John 3:2)

263

In this passage, John is speaking of the bodily resurrection when we shall enter into full inheritance in Christ. But the translation somewhat blurs the meaning. The verse could be paraphrased:

It has never yet been made manifest what we shall be, but we know that when what we are in Christ is manifested, that it will be out of His likeness, and that this will enable us to see Him as He is.

This is based on the original Greek (per M.R. Vincent). It is an awesome thought. If you think about this, it means that what will be manifested is the new creature that we are in Christ – Christ FULLY manifested through us -- without the limits of the natural.

This is the same Truths as found in I Corinthians:

For now we see through a glass, darkly; but then face to face: now I know in part; but then shall I know even as also I am known. (I Cor. 13:12)

Eye has not seen, nor ear heard, neither have entered into the heart of man, the things which God hath prepared for them that love him. (I Cor. 2:9)

All of this is what God has purposed for sons and daughters in Christ. It is the reason for which He has saved humanity. It is why He is speaking to His people in the Person of His Son. And it is also why the New Testament is adamant about keeping Jesus Christ as our life.

The Seed of Abraham

Sonship and inheritance was promised by God through Abraham.

Now to Abraham and his seed were the promises made. He said not, And to seeds, as of many; but as of one, And to thy seed, which is Christ. (Gal. 3:16)

In this verse, we see confirmed the Truth that there are not multiple sons and daughters of God – but ultimately there is only ONE: Jesus Christ. He is THE SON – He is THE SEED of Abraham. Paul makes sure of that. But then he goes on to show the place of the saints:

For ye are all the children of God by faith in Christ Jesus. For as many of you as have been baptized into Christ have put on Christ. There is neither Jew nor Greek, there is neither bond nor free, there is neither male nor female: for ye are all one in Christ Jesus. And if ye [be] Christ's, then are ye Abraham's seed, and heirs according to the promise. (Gal. 3:26-29)

The point Paul makes is that there is one seed of Abraham – one Son of God – but that the saints are sons and daughters IN the Son. The saints IN the Son are collectively the seed of Abraham by virtue of being one with Christ in spirit. Everything a believer is before the Lord, and everything that the believer is to receive, is given solely IN Christ, THROUGH Christ, and by spiritual union WITH CHRIST. In short, God has not so much given us THINGS. He has given us Christ, in Whom are all things. (Rom. 8:32)

The Son of Man

The Son of God became a human being so that human beings could become sons and daughters of God in Him. Unless Jesus had become human He could not have died for humanity. There would be no redemption, no sonship, and consequently, no eternal inheritance.

Much teaching suggests that Jesus died to deliver us from the anger of His Father. God, now appeased, was supposedly set free to love humanity. Such teaching is not only a misrepresentation of the redemption, but it is a misrepresentation of God Himself.

In Truth, Jesus died to deliver us from sin. He died to set US free from this fallen creation. That was made possible when He became human. As the God-man – as the Last Adam, Jesus bore the Adam race on the Cross down into the necessary death because of sin. Those who believe are raised in Christ and saved.

Once Jesus died, and was raised, He ascended into the heavenlies where He is seated at the right hand of God as Lord above all – as The Son who is heir of all things. Yet because we are IN Christ, we are seated IN HIM. Because He inherited all, we inherit all IN HIM. This is possible only because the Son of God became a man and gave Himself for us.

266

That in the dispensation of the fullness of times he might gather together in one all things in Christ, both which are in heaven, and which are on earth; [even] in him: In whom also we have obtained an inheritance, being predestinated according to the purpose of him who works all things after the counsel of his own will. (Eph. 1:10-11)

God is speaking Christ. That is His ONLY Word. It is His complete Word. It is His final Word. In Christ, is revealed, and is given all that God has to give. Unless we see and live in this Truth, we are going to be deceived.

Chapter 32
The Fullness of Him that Fills All in All

The working of His mighty power which he wrought in Christ, when he raised him from the dead, and set [him] at his own right hand in the heavenly [places], Far above all principality, and power, and might, and dominion, and every name that is named, not only in this world, but also in that which is to come: And hath put all [things] under his feet, and gave him [to be] the head over all [things] to the church, Which is his body, the fullness of him that fills all in all. (Eph. 1:19-23)

In the above passage, Paul makes an incredible statement about the church – about, "the called out ones." He says, in verse 23, "The church is His body -- the fullness of Him who fills all in all."

Well, obviously, this is not speaking of anything we will see with our eyes NOW. We do not see a church NOW that is a FULL EXPRESSION of Jesus Christ. In fact, this has NEVER existed. Not even in the first century. There have been various congregations throughout the centuries that have rightly represented Jesus Christ. But, "the fullness of Him that fills all in all?" I don't think so.

But does that mean that God is defeated? No. For even though we will not, in this age, see the church operating as a full expression of Jesus Christ, Jesus is going to have it in the next age.

One reason why the full expression of Christ will only take place through the body of Christ in the next age is that there are millions of members of His body that have passed away. They can no longer operate as part of the expression of Christ – not until the next age. Besides, there is no reason to assume that Paul is talking about the body of Christ during this age. He is most likely talking about the next age.

Individuals will only realize full redemption in Christ at the resurrection of the body at the return of Christ. And since the church is comprised of those individual members it is clear that the realization of the Body of Christ as the full expression of Christ can only begin at that point as well. Thus, is it NOW that God is bringing individuals into an inward realization of Jesus Christ, and in doing so, building the people who constitute His church – but this is all UNTO the full release of His purpose at the resurrection when Christ returns.

We must grasp this: God is NOW building the people who constitute the church – by bringing those individuals into an inward realization of Jesus Christ. But even though there is to be an impact of that in the here and now – it is unto the greater purposes of God in the eternal ages.

The Body of Christ

Believers are all one in Christ -- howbeit scattered geographically and separated by thousands of years over time. Regardless, God is going to gather all of His Body up in Christ. All will be part of the fullness of the expression of Christ. Even though, yes, we, as individuals, can be an individual expression of Christ, it takes the Body to have a full orbed expression of Him. Just as God gives gifts to one that He may not give to another, and just as we have different functions as part of the body, when Christ comes back, all believers gathered together will be the fullness of expression of the Person of Jesus Christ.

Inheritance and Dominion in Christ

Jesus Christ – living in and expressed through individual human beings – but all unto a living expression of Christ through the Body of Christ. This is God's purpose -- that, "He has purposed in Himself." It is the purpose for which He sent Jesus to captain and author. It is why He sent the Son of God to become a man – so that man could be joined to God. That is eternal inheritance – it is our inheritance in God, and it is God's inheritance in the saints.

Herein we see the real meaning of, "reigning and ruling," with Christ. In Ephesians, Paul lays down the fact that Christ is seated at the right hand of God – but he prays that God would give to us a spirit of wisdom and revelation in the knowledge of Himself -- so that we may understand what that really MEANS. Ephesians 2:6 tells us what it means:

We are raised up together and made to sit together in heavenly places in Christ Jesus.

270

If Christ is seated at the right hand of God in heavenly places, then because we are joined to Him, we are seated IN HIM in heavenly places at the right hand of God. We are seated IN CHRIST far above all principality, might and dominion.

That word, "dominion," is very important with regard to God's purpose for humanity. God created humanity to, "have dominion," under Himself over God's creation. His purpose for humanity has never been changed. It is now to be undertaken and fulfilled in and through Christ – Christ as THE SON OF MAN -- and then, by extension -- through humanity that is joined to Christ.

So, what we see is that at the root of, "reigning and ruling," with Christ is the fact that we are joined to Him – and therefore operating IN HIM, and as an EXTENTION of Him.

Contrast this over and against the mistaken notion that Jesus sort of hands us authority and power to rule over nations and people – howbeit in His name. No. We are joined to the Lord. We are members of HIS BODY. The picture is impossible to escape. We reign and rule with Christ in the sense that He reigns and rules – FIRST IN US – but then through us. We are expressions and extensions of the Living Christ unto others.

As noted, this can happen to a certain degree NOW with individuals, and even with congregations. But we do not see it much. The fullness of it can only happen with the entire church that Jesus is building being united through the resurrection from the dead.

Inheritance and Sonship

We have already discussed sonship and inheritance. Certainly that is central to what we are talking about here. In that prior discussion we noted that we can summarize sonship and God's inheritance plan in this way:

The Father

The Only or Uniquely Begotten Son

and

All who are IN the Son.

That is inheritance. But it is also dominion as well because a part of inheritance is to have dominion. If you go all the way back into the Book of Genesis, you see that God created man to have dominion. If we read, for example, Genesis 1:26, God says, "Let us make man in our image and let him have dominion over all of the creatures of the earth..." It says later on in that chapter that God blessed them and said to them, "Be fruitful and multiply and replenish the earth and subdue it and have dominion over..."

We can turn to the NT and see this same purpose that God had for humanity clearly stated. In Hebrews 2:5:

For unto the angels God has not put into subjection the world to come whereof we

speak. But one, in a certain place, testified saying, "What is man that Thou art mindful of him or the son of man that Thou visit him? You made him a little lower than the angels. You crowned him with glory and honor and did set him over the works of your hands. You have put all things in subjection under his feet. In that He put all under subjection to him, he left nothing which is not under subjection to him. But now we see not all things yet put under him -- BUT we see Jesus.

We have here, from out of Psalm 8, the purpose of God stated for which He created humanity: To put all of God's creation in subjection under humanity. This passage clearly states that presently, in this age, we don't see much of this – certainly not the way God intended. In fact, we see much the opposite. BUT -- what we do see is **THE MAN** through Whom this purpose of God will come to pass – and **THE MAN** through Whom the rest of humanity – those who accept Christ -- will be able to realize it: We see **THE MAN** – the God-man – JESUS CHRIST.

Yes. "We see Jesus, who was made a little lower than the angels, through the suffering of death was crowned with glory and honor, that He, by the grace of God should taste death for every man." What we are seeing here is that Adam's sin caused him to lose dominion. But God sent His Son as THE MAN – the Last Adam -- who would win back all things under the lordship of His Father. We SEE JESUS – and once we have Him revealed in us we can begin to see this great purpose of God through Him.

273

The Son of God become man is the One through Whom God will accomplish all. There was no salvation for humanity unless Jesus became a member of the human race. God had to become man so that man could be joined to God. Therefore, there could not be the fulfillment of God's purpose for humanity unless Jesus became a member of the human race.

Gather this up and you discover that IN CHRIST humanity has dominion restored. But as noted, it is vital to understand that we are not given dominion or anything else of God, "in addition to Christ," or, "tacked onto Christ," or even as a separate thing because of what Christ did for us. No. We are given CHRIST HIMSELF. And because we are given Christ Himself, then we have been given ALL that is IN HIM – which includes dominion.

Note Revelation 3:21, where Jesus says, "He that overcomes will I grant to sit with Me in My throne, even as I also overcame and sat down with My Father in His throne." There is no picture there of the believer being given a throne of his own in addition to the throne of Christ. No. We do not possess a little throne -- as compared to Jesus' big throne. Rather, Christ sits in His throne and we are given the opportunity to sit IN HIM in His throne. In other words, there is ONE throne. We are coheirs with Christ. We reign and rule only IN Him. We are given Christ, in whom God has given all else. It is only by living in Him and being in subjection to Him that we have dominion over what He has dominion over. This is God's purpose.

This ought to all the more emphasize why it is vital to see that Christ is ALL to the believer. It is why we must see that He is our life. There is nothing God does that is independent of Christ. We have all – but only in Him. In HIM we live and move and have our being. And as it pertains to the eternal ages, He lives and moves in and through His body.

Obviously, Jesus Christ does not need us. But God has purposed to created humanity to bestow upon us this incredible gift.

This takes us back to what we saw in Ephesians 1. God is calling people out of this world to His Son. By coming to Jesus, we can be adopted as sons and daughters IN the Son. But in the Bible, adoption did not mean what it means today. In that day, to be adopted as a child meant that you had to FIRST be born into the family – and then later you could be adopted. You could be adopted -- made a child in that family – made an heir -- only if you proved yourself able to be responsible for the inheritance. God has called us to Christ that we should come to the point where they we can be adopted as sons and daughters in Jesus Christ – and thus become coheirs with Him; reign and rule with Him.

Paul uses other terms to explain the same Truth in Galatians. He declares that there is only ONE seed of Abraham: Jesus Christ. But because we are in Him and have become one with Him, we are also collectively in Him the seed of Abraham. And the seed of Abraham is the one to whom all the inheritance and dominion is given.

God's Inheritance in the Saints

That ye may know what is the hope of his calling, and what is the riches of the glory of his inheritance in the saints. (Eph. 1:18)

Giving thanks unto the Father, which hath made us meet to be partakers of the inheritance of the saints in light. (Col. 1:12)

The Bible reveals much about the inheritance of the saints in Christ. But here we find mention of God's inheritance in the saints. The only difference between the two is the direction in which this inheritance flows. The inheritance of the saints in Christ flows from Christ to the saints. The inheritance of God in the saints flows from Christ to the Father. Either way, the One in Whom all inheritance is vested is Jesus Christ. Jesus Christ IN God's people is both the saint's inheritance in Christ, and God's inheritance in the saints.

Earlier we saw the inheritance described in Ephesians:

That in the dispensation of the fullness of times he might gather together in one all things in Christ, both which are in heaven, and which are on earth; [even] in him. (Eph. 1:10)

And hath put all [things] under his feet, and gave him [to be] the head over all [things] to the church, Which is his body,

the fullness of him that fills all in all. (Eph. 1:22-23)

God's inheritance and the inheritance of the is to have a people in and through Whom His Son will be manifested. They will be a people who are expressions and extensions of Christ — all unto God's glory.

We have already seen that sonship and inheritance are possible ONLY because The Son of God became a human being. It was because God became man that man can be made one with God through Him. So again, God's plan of inheritance is: The Father, the Son, and all who are in the Son.

Chapter 33
The Alpha and the Omega

I am Alpha and Omega, the beginning and the end, the first and the last. (Rev. 22:13)

Earlier we read Paul's immense declaration of the purpose of God: That in the fullness of time, God was going to gather up all things in Christ -- and that He would be the head over all things to the church, which is His Body, "the fullness of Him who fills all in all." What we see is that God, in this age, is calling a people to Himself, in His Son -- so that those people in Christ might be an expression of Himself. And -- that Christ might live and work through them to do His will.

The full realization of this purpose will be in the next age. But there will be impacts, workings, and manifestations of this purpose in this age. For Christ does dwell in His people. And wherever the presence of Christ is allowed to be manifested through those people there is going to be an impact. We see this in the book of Acts. And if Christ had freedom in His people in this age, we would see more of it today.

In this age, God is working from the inside out. Christ must first be formed and realized IN God's people before He can be manifested through them. This is a foundational Truth that applies to all that God has given in Christ, and to all that God wants to do through Christ. It applies to all ministry, all dominion, all power, and to all of life in Christ. For Christ IS the Life, the Truth, and the Power of God. He is that in

Himself – and wants to be that both IN and THROUGH His people.

Jesus said, "I am Alpha and Omega." He also wants to be that in us by experience. This is simply another way of describing Jesus Christ as Lord of all.

The Members of His Body

So, God has called a Body now -- to give themselves over to His Son -- so that He is able to live through them. In short, the Body ought to live and express Christ – ought to do things that He would do if He were here. That is what a body does! Again, we do not see much of this today; we don't see a lot of public demonstration of these things. (We do see a lot of fake things!) But the real begins with Christ in us working from the inside out to the point where He can live through His Body.

Many of us have blinded by tradition and human thinking on these matters. One of the biggest mistakes we make is to assume that the plan of God is going to be fully realized in THIS age. It is NOT. This age is the age of planting seeds. It is the age of laying foundations. It is the age of preparation. It is the age of separating the wheat from the tares. And of course, it is the age of suffering and adversity. It is only in the NEXT AGE after Christ returns that the actual FRUITAGE of what God is doing in this age is going to be seen and expressed fully. And God wants to express that fruitage through the Body of Christ.

The Unseen Realm

We have dominion, in Christ, over the power of the enemy – because we are one with the resurrection life of Christ. But there are going to be many seasons where it does not seem like it. It may seem as if nothing ever happens, and there will come a temptation of doubt.

We need to realize that most of the spiritual impact of Jesus Christ is in the spiritual realm. Indeed, if there is no impact of Christ THERE – then there isn't going to be any lasting impact at all. As we have seen, God works from the inside out – He works through the spiritual first. We are blessed in Christ with all spiritual blessings in the HEAVENLIES. We are seated with Christ in the HEAVENLIES. That is where things begin and are the most important. And we cannot see with our eyes, nor feel with our emotions, the HEAVENLIES.

Two verses elsewhere in Ephesians will suffice to emphasize that it is in the unseen spiritual realm that the greatest impact of Christ is realized:

For we wrestle not against flesh and blood, but against principalities, against powers, against the rulers of the darkness of this world, against spiritual wickedness in high [places]. (Eph. 6:10)

That I should preach among the Gentiles the unsearchable riches of Christ; And to make all [men] see what [is] the fellowship of the mystery, which from the beginning of the world hath been hid in God, who created

all things by Jesus Christ: To the intent that now unto the principalities and powers in heavenly [places] might be known by the church the manifold wisdom of God. (Eph. 3:8-10)

We wrestle not against flesh and blood – things we can see. But we wrestle against forces we cannot see. In addition, through the church, God is judging these same evil forces. We cannot gain access through natural senses or emotions to any of this. But nevertheless in Christ there is a great impact. That impact is negative to the evil one. But it is positive in Christ.

There are times when you can discern that something happened spiritually. There are other times when you cannot. But this is NOT about your ability to discern. It is about being those who are seated with Christ and given the responsibility to live in Him.

If you are walking with Jesus and letting Him have you, then you may not see outward evidence of any impact -- but there is one because you are living from the throne. You are seated with Christ in the heavenlies and you are praying according to the will of God. That moves things and things do happen in the spirit. You may never see them but it does not change the fact.

For His Body's Sake

There is nothing about US – within ourselves – that we can contribute to the body of Christ. But by giving ourselves individually to Christ, His life can be contributed to others in the body.   Paul taught this great Truth. He said:

But we have this treasure in earthen vessels, that the excellency of the power may be of God, and not of us. [We are] troubled on every side, yet not distressed; [we are] perplexed, but not in despair; Persecuted, but not forsaken; cast down, but not destroyed; Always bearing about in the body the dying of the Lord Jesus, that the life also of Jesus might be made manifest in our body. For we which live are always delivered unto death for Jesus' sake, that the life also of Jesus might be made manifest in our mortal flesh. So then death worketh in us, but life in you. (II Cor. 4:7-12)

"Death in us, but life in you."   That is spiritual ministry.   But that would make absolutely no sense unless we are members of one another. In other words, we are individually joined to Christ in resurrection union – but because we are individually joined to the same Christ, it is therefore a fact that THROUGH HIM joined to one another.   That is why Paul wrote that if one member suffers, all suffer.   That is the meaning of COMMUNION – "a having in common."   We have Christ in common – not just as the One who saved each of us – but we have Him in common in that HE IS OUR COMMON LIFE.

So we see that each individual believer is ONE in spirit with Jesus Christ. But likewise, because we are one in spirit with Christ, each individual believer is ONE in spirit with other believers –

regardless of whether we attend church. The ramifications of this Truth often take place in the spiritual realm. For example, yes, God is doing a work in you and I personally and individually. But that work that is being done in us is NOT JUST FOR US. No. God is creating in EACH believer something that will contribute to the spiritual life of all other believers. "Death in us, but life in you." And again, this is not merely for here, in this age – but more so for the eternal ages.

Obviously, what God does in the individual is for His purpose in that individual. That is primary. But we are members of one another. And so what God does is going to INDIRECTLY be a contribution to the rest of the body of Christ. It will be a contribution to the body whether we attend church or not; whether that contribution is presently seen or not in this age.

We must also remember that the body of Christ is comprised of ALL who have even been in Christ – those who are alive and dead in Jesus are ALL ONE in Him. But only a small part of His body is physically alive at any one time. Consequently, if the entire body is to benefit from the life of Christ in one member then it will have to be, not in this age, but in the age to come, that the fullness of what God is doing can be manifested. Thus, again -- all that God is doing in individuals will only be realized when the entire body is gathered up and assembled together in Christ at His second coming.

Paul's Ministry

Paul wrote:

> *I, Paul am made a minister;   Who now rejoice in my sufferings for you, and fill up that which is behind of the afflictions of Christ in my flesh for his body's sake, which is the church: (Col. 1:23-24)*

Paul was the one who wrote, "Death in us, but life in you."   This passage expands upon that declaration.   He clearly states that he suffers, "for His body's sake."   It is a part of what ministry IS — to allow Jesus Christ to do in you that which not only ministers to others, but that which Christ desires to do in others.   Those other members of the body may never meet you or know your name.   But what Christ has in you will contribute to what Christ has in them.

Now, all of this during this age is merely a foretaste — a preparation for — what God intends to have in the body of Christ during the next age.   God wants a body of Christ that operates in complete harmony with the Head.   He wants a people who are utterly abandoned to Jesus Christ.   Those people not only will do the will of God, but will BE the will of God.   They will be both expressions and extensions of the Living Christ.

The Ages to Come

God has not revealed many specifics about the eternal ages — except that it will be beyond what we can comprehend with our natural minds — and even then that is stated in general terms:

284

Eye hath not seen, nor ear heard, neither have entered into the heart of man, the things which God hath prepared for them that love him. (I Cor. 2:9)

For I reckon that the sufferings of this present time [are] not worthy [to be compared] with the glory which shall be revealed in us. For the earnest expectation of the creature waits for the manifestation of the sons of God. For the creature was made subject to vanity, not willingly, but by reason of him who hath subjected [the same] in hope, Because the creature itself also shall be delivered from the bondage of corruption into the glorious liberty of the children of God. For we know that the whole creation groans and travails in pain together until now. And not only [they], but ourselves also, which have the first fruits of the Spirit, even we ourselves groan within ourselves, waiting for the adoption, [to wit], the redemption of our body. (Rom. 8:18-23)

There is also this proclamation by Paul:

And hath raised [us] up together, and made [us] sit together in heavenly [places] in Christ Jesus: That in the ages to come he might show the exceeding riches of his grace in [his] kindness toward us through Christ Jesus. (Eph. 2:6-7)

When everything is said and done, those who are in Christ remain recipients of His grace. It is grace by which God does all things in His Son during this age, and it is grace by which God will do all things in the ages to come.

The New Jerusalem

John, as recorded in Revelation, saw a vision that he called, "The New Jerusalem:

And I John saw the holy city, new Jerusalem, coming down from God out of heaven, prepared as a bride adorned for her husband. And I heard a great voice out of heaven saying, Behold, the tabernacle of God [is] with men, and he will dwell with them, and they shall be his people, and God himself shall be with them, [and be] their God. (Rev. 21:2-3)

What is The New Jerusalem? First of all, it is NOT a literal city. Rather, it is the spiritual dwelling place IN CHRIST. The New Jerusalem is resurrection union between Jesus Christ and His people. It is the fullness of, "Christ in you." (Col. 1:27)

Another way to state the same Truth is this: The New Jerusalem is not a heavenly city. Rather, it is a heavenly people. The New Jerusalem consists of those who are IN CHRIST. Believers are joined to the Lord and one spirit with Him. (I Cor. 6:17) That spiritual, resurrection union – comprised of all who are of the church – is The New Jerusalem. This is the, "city that has foundations, whose builder and maker is God." (Heb. 11:10)

286

This is verified every place in the NT where The New Jerusalem is mentioned or suggested -- for example, another reference in the Book of Revelation:

Him that overcomes will I make a pillar in the temple of my God, and he shall go no more out: and I will write upon him the name of my God, and the name of the city of my God, which is new Jerusalem, which cometh down out of heaven from my God: and [I will write upon him] my new name. He that hath an ear, let him hear what the Spirit says unto the churches. (Rev. 3:12-13)

INDIVIDUALS in Christ comprise the body of Christ, and thus, individuals in union with Christ constitute The New Jerusalem.

You will note that The New Jerusalem is, "the city of my God" – and it comes, "down out of heaven from my God." What we see here is that The New Jerusalem is heavenly or spiritual in nature – it comes down and IS from above; from the heavenly realm. More than that, it comes from out from God Himself – it is of HIS mind, indeed, of His very life. The life source of The New Jerusalem is God Himself through His Son.

Christianity is CHRIST IN US (Col. 1:27), and a Christian is one in whom Christ dwells. A Christian is one who, "is joined to the Lord and made one spirit with Him." (I Cor. 6:17) That is HOW Christ dwells in the believer – through spiritual union. These Truths correspond exactly with John's vision – "The dwelling place of God is

287

with men. He will dwell with them; God Himself shall be with them. The New Jerusalem is the representation of God dwelling IN humanity. Sure. God has taken up residence in humanity through His Son. This is Christ in us and The New Jerusalem.

The fact that Abraham was, even in His time, looking for a city, tells us that CHRIST IN US was the purpose of God — was the, "city that has foundations" -- that God was building this, "city," from the start.

This has eternal ramifications — it is central to what He is doing. God the Father is revealing His Son in people; God is building Christ in people, and bringing them into an inward realization of Jesus. This is Redemption. It is fundamental to God bringing all creation under Jesus Christ as Lord.

Chapter 34
The Realization of His Glory

Earlier, we touched on a passage that merits a bit more discussion – because it captures the purpose of God for the redeemed:

Beloved, now are we the sons of God, and it does not yet appear what we shall be: but we know that when he shall appear, we shall be like him; for we shall see him as he is. (1 John 3:2)

We also noted that this verse could be paraphrased:

It has never yet been made manifest what we shall be, but we know that when what we are in Christ is manifested, that it will be out of His likeness, and that this will enable us to see Him as He is.

Link this up with another passage that is talking about the same Truth:

For we must all appear before the judgment seat of Christ; that every one may receive the things [done] in [his] body, according to that he hath done, whether [it be] good or bad. (II Cor. 5:10)

This ought to read:

For we must all be made manifest by the judgment seat of Christ...

Now, let's add the second part of the verse the way it ought to read:

...that every one may receive THRU BODY according to that which he hath done, whether good or bad.

These two passages are giving us a peak at the relationship between what Jesus Christ is doing in His people NOW — and how that is going to be released at the resurrection into the eternal ages. If we were to gather up this Truth and summarize it in one statement we might say:

In this age, Christianity is, "Christ in you, the hope of His glory." At the resurrection, it will be, "Christ in you, the realization of His glory."

Human beings were created to both receive, and then be manifestations, of God's glory. We are never given a glory of our own. But to experience the glory of Jesus Christ — that simply means that we are destined to experience all that Jesus Christ IS.

You will also note that the reward of the saints is not THINGS. It is not first of all, "positions," or rulership OVER people or nations. Rather, the reward of the saints is Christ Himself — the eternal experiencing and living in His glory.

How does one come into this reward? Not by works. Not by service. Not by following a list of principles designed to, "built Christian character." No. A Christian person come to where they can fully live in and experience Jesus Christ THEN, by living in, and experiencing Christ NOW.

This means we, "walk in the light as He is in the light." We all have SOME light – some knowledge of Jesus Christ. We need to walk with Him in it.

We need not compare ourselves to others, and we need to turn our eyes inwardly upon ourselves. This is not a contest or competition. It is a living fellowship. Read the parables of Jesus. We are responsible for ourselves before God regarding what we have been given.

In this age, God is planting seeds. He is establishing foundations for relationship. What little faith God is able to prove in us NOW, will have eternal ramifications THEN. We cannot know the beginning from the end on these matters. But we can walk by faith in Christ and leave all of that to Him.

The primary way in which we are to walk in the light with Jesus Christ now is by abandoning ourselves to Jesus Christ by faith -- and by asking Him to do, "whatever it takes," to bring us on. Then as He does do, "whatever it takes," we walk with Him.

This is not opinion. It is exactly what Jesus stated to His disciples:

If any [man] will come after me, let him deny himself, and take up his cross, and follow me. For whosoever will save his life shall lose it: and whosoever will lose his life for my sake shall find it. (Matt: 16:24-25)

You do not hear much preaching about this verse. But if you do hear some, it is usually made to mean, "Believe Jesus died for you on the Cross." That is missing the entire point. Jesus said, "IF anyone would come after ME…." That is the Christian walk; the Christian life. And it involves a PERSONAL Cross.

Paul wrote:

I am crucified with Christ: nevertheless I live; yet not I, but Christ lives in me: and the life which I now live in the flesh I live by the faith of the Son of God, who loved me, and gave himself for me. (Gal. 2:20)

Jesus Christ died for each of us. But it is because He died for each of us, that each of us can now DIE IN HIM. And according to Paul, this is the necessity for freedom from sin.

Knowing this, that our old man is crucified with [him], that the body of sin might be destroyed, that henceforth we should not serve sin. 7 For he that is dead is freed from sin. Now if we be dead with Christ, we believe that we shall also live with him: Knowing that Christ being raised from the dead dieth no more; death hath no more dominion over him. For in that he died, he died unto sin once: but in that he liveth, he liveth unto God. Likewise reckon ye also yourselves to be dead indeed unto sin, but alive unto God through Jesus Christ our

Lord. Let not sin therefore reign in your mortal body, that ye should obey it in the lusts thereof. (Rom.6:6-12)

This, and many other passages in the NT, reveal that the personal Cross is the key to freedom FROM sin – but also the key to true life in Jesus Christ NOW. And as we have seen, that has an impact upon life in Christ THEN, in the eternal ages.

Freely Given

Freely ye have received, freely give. (Matt. 10:8)

Jesus gave this command as He was about to send out His disciples for the first time to minister in His name. In a very real sense, this one, simple sentence, captures the spirit of Christianity. Christianity is GRACE. God is the God of all grace. All that God does is by His grace, and thus, all that we do in His name, must be nothing more than that same grace given through us.

God has freely given all things IN HIS SON – He has freely given Christ Himself. (Rom. 8:32) We can only receive that which God has freely given – by freely receiving. God gives by grace, and we received by grace. No strings attached. But then, we are to give back to God, and give to others, FREELY. It is all of grace.

This will be the ONLY life that emerges from abandoning ourselves to Jesus Christ. It is what the personal Cross produces: A person who is able to freely received from God, and a person who is able to freely give of themselves out from what they have freely received from God. And in the final analysis, all that is freely given, received, and then again given, is of Jesus Christ.

This is the essence of the eternal relationship for which God is in this age is seeking to establish in His people: Grace. Love. Truth. It is the outcome of REDEMPTION.

www.goodnewsaudio.com

www.goodnewsarticles.com

Made in the USA
Middletown, DE
07 June 2023

32196606R00166